The Death of French Culture

The Death of French Culture

Donald Morrison
and
Antoine Compagnon

Response by Antoine Compagnon translated
by Andrew Brown

polity

First published in French as *Que reste-t-il de la culture française?* suivi de *Le souci de la grandeur* © Éditions Denoël, 2008

This English edition © Polity Press, 2010
Reprinted 2010

Polity Press
65 Bridge Street
Cambridge CB2 1UR, UK

Polity Press
350 Main Street
Malden, MA 02148, USA

ISBN-13: 978-0-7456-4993-1 (hardback)
ISBN-13: 978-0-7456-4994-8 (paperback)

A catalogue record for this book is available from the British Library.

Typeset in 11 on 13 pt Sabon
by Toppan Best-set Premedia Limited
Printed and bound in Great Britain by the MPG Books Group

The publisher has used its best endeavours to ensure that the URLs for external websites referred to in this book are correct and active at the time of going to press. However, the publisher has no responsibility for the websites and can make no guarantee that a site will remain live or that the content is or will remain appropriate.

For further information on Polity, visit our website:
www.politybooks.com

Contents

1

The Death of French Culture

Donald Morrison

I.

Hollywood has a bad reputation among the French. They
tend to equate the U.S. movie capital with formulaic thrillers,
overmarketed blockbusters, glitzy special effects, and gratui-
tous violence. But Hollywood's untold secret is that most
of the 500 or so feature films it turns out every year are
modestly budgeted productions, many of them intelligent
and original.

Consider director Ridley Scott's 1991 female-buddy picture
Thelma and Louise. It cost a relatively low 16 million dollars
to make and was nominated for six Oscars (winning one, for
best screenplay), eight British BAFTAs and a French César.
Like any good movie, *Thelma and Louise* has its share of
surprises. In a pivotal scene, for instance, Louise (Susan
Sarandon) confronts a man who has just sexually assaulted
her friend Thelma (Gina Davis) in a parking lot. The man
laughs at Louise's feeble attempts to intervene.

So she pulls out a gun and shoots him dead. Says a flab-
bergasted Thelma: "I bet he didn't expect *that*."

I know how he feels. There I was minding my own
business – or, rather, France's – when the fury of Gallic
public opinion hit me in the sternum like Louise's unexpected

The Death of French Culture

bullet. I should have seen it coming. I should have realized that an American cannot make unwanted advances on the power and glory of French culture without provoking a sharp and unpleasant response. I would have been wise to confine my thoughts on the subject to Paris dinner parties and e-mails to friends back home, rather than publishing an article entitled "The Death of French Culture" in an American magazine. But I was under the delusion that my remarks would be perceived by French readers much as I perceived them: as friendly, positive observations about a country I rather like.

How naïve, how obtuse, how American. Didn't I know that culture is the sacred *vache* of French public life, the soft and easily irritated underbelly of national self-regard? You can criticize France's work ethic, its smoking habits, its tax régime. But whatever you do, don't say anything bad about its culture. And do not for a moment think that your observations will be taken lightly, your criticisms considered constructive. Don't expect people to understand that you were just trying to help. When a foreigner tries to help by pointing out certain, ahem ... shortcomings in the realm of French culture, his good deed does not go unpunished.

My punishment was swift and public. Within days after my 3,000-word article on the decline of France as an international cultural power appeared in *Time* magazine's December 3, 2007, European edition, the French media lit up like the Eiffel Tower in full sparkle.[1] Nearly every major daily newspaper, broadcast channel, and serious website in the country carried a report on my impertinence. Government officials, cultural mandarins, and the media outlets' own culture reporters were trotted out to refute my assertions. A typical response, by *Le Nouvel Observateur* literary columnist Didier Jacob: "For Americans, French culture is simultaneously an object of derision and desire. If there were an algebraic formula to sum up its quintessence, it would go a little like this: De Gaulle + Sartre + the baguette + Sophie Marceau's breasts = French culture." Jacob's observation, posted on the magazine's website, prompted dozens of responses. Many were of this sort: "I don't know the author of this article, but he can't possibly be serious."

"The U.S. counts among its populace many researchers, scholars, thinkers and innovators of the highest level. Only, they don't write for *Time*," sneered Maurice Druon, the grand old man of French letters, in *Le Figaro*. He accused me of having confused, "like the majority of his public, culture and entertainment." (Where he found time to interview all of my public, I know not.) Druon's polemic was accompanied by no fewer than five articles in a valiantly jingoistic attempt by *Le Figaro* to eviscerate my opus. The newspaper dispatched its correspondents in the U.S. to find evidence that French culture was thriving there, though they did not detect much activity outside New York City. Other *Le Figaro* journalists reported that French painters were doing well in London, that French philosophers were held in high respect around the world (though, for some reason, not French novelists), that French architects were thriving and that French films were popular everywhere except, um . . . outside France. *Le Figaro*'s campaign – spread over three pages, with nice photos of the French techno-pop group Daft Punk in funny hats and of Bartabas, creator of the "equestrian theater" Zingaro, posing with one of his horses – seemed like overkill. Was *Le Figaro* subliminally acknowledging that I had hit a sensitive nerve?

Still in *Le Figaro*, art dealer Anne Faggionato noted that my article contained lots of facts and complained that "All these pseudo-analyses in the American style try to legitimize themselves by citing numbers. But art can't be measured that way, its econometrics are absurd, and the future will prove its worth." In *Libération*, Teresa Cremisi, chief executive of the Flammarion publishing house, deplored my "mercantilist" view in which culture is seen solely in terms of immediate returns. A few French came to my defense, most admirably the hot young novelist David Foenkinos, who told *Le Nouvel Observateur*: "Fundamentally, Morrison isn't wrong. I believe the cultural power of France is in decline, that's evident to me. History is full of periods, hegemonies and round-trips."

The blogosphere went into overdrive, as websites from Bibliobs.fr to the Vietnamese-language Diendan.org saw fit to comment on the story. A posting on Superfrenchie.com received 165 responses, most of them chastising me for various errors and omissions. Even critics outside France weighed in. American author Edward Champion called me "*Time Magazine*'s cultural answer to Fox News," a wounding insult to any serious journalist. Champion further suggested that "Morrison doesn't know what the fuck he's talking about." With equal delicacy, a reader of British pop-culture critic Momus' website posted this penetrating observation: "Morrison really shat the bed. Embarrassing. Fortunately, *Time* can't even get noticed in the waiting room of the average dentist's office these days."

The foreign press quickly picked up on the controversy. The London *Times*' man in Paris, Charles Bremner, asserted that I had overstated France's failings. Britain's *Guardian* went so far as to commission a critique from Bernard-Henri Lévy, the leading French celebrity-intellectual, who observed that my article was less about France's decline than America's. Declared journalist Iman Kurdi in Saudi Arabia's *Arab News*: "I not only disagree [with Morrison] but cheer the fact that France has remained distinctly French." I did better in the *Financial Times*, where columnist Christopher Caldwell used my assertions as a springboard for a critique of French lip service toward cultural diversity. Perhaps the most admiring of my critics was Catherine Fieschi, director of the British Council think tank Counterpoint. Writing in *Prospect* magazine, she congratulated me for having "lobbed a small hand grenade into the playground of the French intelligentsia."

I got to confront some of that playground's habitants directly. Two French TV programs allowed me to debate Olivier Poivre d'Arvor, the head of the Foreign Ministry-financed Culturesfrance and author of a *Le Monde* article questioning my conclusions. (He was thoughtful and gracious, on-air and off.) I participated in yet another TV chat with film director Constantin Costa-Gavras (*Z, Missing, State of Siege*), editor François Busnel of the book-lovers' magazine *Lire*, and cultural commentators Jérôme Béglé and Frédéric Martel. A few of these experts found things to admire in my story; all of them spotted grave deficiencies in it.

My own country's Ambassador to France, Craig Stapleton, wrote a letter to the editor of *Time* about the controversy. But instead of standing up for me, Stapleton leapt to the defense of France, which, in the America of his boss George W. Bush, was not enormously popular at the time. Wrote Stapleton: "The vitality of French culture should be measured by more than just the box-office receipts of the week." That is not quite how I measured things, but most commentators seemed not to have noticed, contenting themselves with righteous indignation at my supposed attack on the glory that was France.

I was, frankly, astonished at the size and passion of the response I had provoked. So were some of my detractors. Wrote author and critic Pierre Assouline: "How an article like this can inspire such an outburst of anger in the French media, and provoke such fistfights in the blogosphere, is a mystery I cannot explain." John Brenkman, a professor at New York City's Baruch College, wondered whether the French were taking the whole thing a bit too seriously. My story, he wrote in *Le Monde*,

> has had, in France, the same result as Orson Welles' 1938 radio adaptation of H. G. Wells' *War of the Worlds*, which announced to America, in realistic and convincing tones, that Martians had invaded. Today, it's the French who have persuaded themselves of an American attack on French culture. . . Put another way, the *Time* article is nothing but a hoax, and the public, egged on by the French media, is the victim. "A sucker is born every day," said P. T. Barnum, the grand man of show business . . . In this case, the sucker – pardon me – is France. You, my French friends, have swallowed it hook, line and sinker.

The Death of French Culture

Amid all the fuss, I flew to New York City for a few days of quiet. The debate raged on without me. My New York trip was interrupted by the BBC, which tracked me down at a Manhattan restaurant. Over the din of clattering dishes and shouting waiters, I went on the air in a live radio debate with the *Independent*'s veteran Paris correspondent, John Lichfield. I couldn't hear very well, so he did most of the talking.

The problem, it seemed, was not so much my article as the cover of the issue in which it appeared. That featured a rather appealing portrait by London-based photographer Pål C. Hansen of the great French mime Marcel Marceau, staring with wistful sadness, as mimes do, at a flower the very same shade as *Time*'s trademark red border. The image was a brilliant choice: Marceau had died a few months earlier, and with him a piece of France's heart – thus underlining the note of loss and poignancy that I had tried to attain in my story. (I was not alone in this view. Olivier Poivre d'Arvor also found Marceau a fitting cover subject: "It is true that over the past few years, for those who do not speak the language, it has been the silent artists of French culture who have hit your headlines: the mime artist Marceau, the silent abysses of Commandant [Jacques] Cousteau, our choreographers, our circus acts . . . We resist, with all our powers, our sublime speechlessness, our faltering discomfort, the uproar and hubbub of the world, but we would still like to impress you, just a little, modestly, in the French style."[2] Poivre d'Arvor, the brother of famed TV presenter Patrick Poivre d'Arvor and the man in charge of promoting French culture abroad, wrote this in a "letter to our American friends" published in *Le Monde*.

In any case, it is a beautiful photograph, clean and simple, classical in composition – and with that vivid red flower to catch the eye. A bit of a cliché, I must admit. Just as the French press has a weakness for depicting Americans in cowboy hats and Englishmen in bowlers, U.S. publications love to put the French in bérets and striped boating shirts. But as a cover image, it certainly jumped off the newsstand.

So, unhappily for me, did the article's headline: "The Death of French Culture." The subhead was equally inflammatory: "Quick, name a living artist or writer from France who has global significance. Right. But help is on the way." I did not write any of those words. On French TV, I joked that, like many American companies, *Time* now outsourced the writing of its cover lines to a call center in India. (No one laughed.) In fact, the words were penned at the magazine's European headquarters in London. I did not see them or the cover image until after they were printed. Frankly, I was rather shocked. My article was not about "death," but rather about decline and redemption. Still unaware of the cover and its headline, I gave an interview to *Libération*. My interviewer, Edouard Launet, had the delicacy not to mention them, but I came away from our chat with an uneasy feeling – justified, as it turned out. In his article, Launet asks peevishly: "What bug bit Don Morrison to make him tear French culture to pieces?"

Me, a shredder of culture, a merchant of pique? I am innocent, I thought. But then I thought again. Having been an editor myself for more than three decades, I have written my share of provocative headlines. I realize that it is sometimes necessary to use inflammatory language on a magazine cover in order to seize the public's attention. Of course it is an exaggeration to say that French culture is dead. But it is a modest and perhaps necessary overstatement if one's task is to grab readers by the lapels. If the hyperbolic language on the cover led the French to wonder why they no longer dominate the cultural landscape, to re-examine the efficacy of their many cultural subsidies and quotas, and to better integrate France's long-excluded minorities into the cultural scene, then so much the better.

And that, in fact, is pretty much what happened. The French cultural establishment spent the next two years not just denouncing me and *Time*, but also re-examining the role of culture in national life. Seemingly endless hours were expended in debates on TV and radio, and hectares of newsprint were lavished on commentaries and responses.

7

The Death of French Culture

Sometimes I was mentioned, often not. The story just wouldn't go away. I hardly expected to be made a Chevalier in the Order of Arts and Letters, but I was gratified by the seriousness with which the French took my musings.

This seriousness was confirmed by Olivier Poivre d'Arvor, who thanked me for "this magnificent cover of *Time*." It presented, he said, a welcome opportunity to reflect on the value of France's cultural assets. He wrote, in an article I arranged to have published in *Time*: "Admittedly, *Time*'s gift was unexpected. Giving such prominence to French culture in its readers' minds rather than issues of worldwide interest. Our fifteen minutes of fame! The chance to remind our fellow countrymen that nothing can be taken for granted, that it is necessary to fight, including at home, to reaffirm the importance of this culture, the power of our influence. A way of reawakening the interest of the political community, the media, the culture professionals and the general public in this exceptional topic . . ." You're welcome, Olivier.

As the reactions poured in, I began to have regrets. My article was too short to explore such a complex subject in sufficient detail. Too much good material had been left on the cutting-room floor. Important points had gone unaddressed, trenchant arguments unmade. The time allotted to me for research, interviews, and reflection had been inadequate. The writing could have been more felicitous. The usual author's regrets.

So I leapt at a French publisher's offer to dilate on the subject at book length. As before, I did not wish to join the crowded field of France-in-decline books, but merely to continue the vigorous debate that the article had inspired and, possibly, to illuminate a path to understanding and renewal. As with my magazine article, this new, expanded version was met with a similar chorus of shock and refutation when it was published in France in late 2008. Another round of TV and newspaper interviews ensued, including a full-page Q.-and-A. in *Le Monde*, a profile as "Person of the Day" in *Libération*, and an invitation to appear on French radio's equivalent of "Desert Island Discs." This time around,

8

however, I had company. To my delight, the eminent scholar Antoine Compagnon had generously agreed to write a response, which is included in this volume. I was, and remain, honored to be in his company.

I am also grateful to the scholars, writers, artists, colleagues, friends, and other *amateurs* of French culture who shared their wisdom and eased my task in many ways. Prominent among them are Frédéric Martel, Guy Walter, Douglas Kennedy, François Busnel, Christophe Boïcos, Marc Lévy, and Georgina Oliver; my *Time* colleagues Claire Senard, Peter Gumbel and Grant Rosenberg (who helped with the reporting); Michael Elliott, William Green, and James Graff (the *Time* trio who commissioned and edited the original article); Yves and Florence Darbois, Jonathan and Renée Fenby, David and Rebecca Tepfer, and Joseph and Sigun Coyle, my advisers on things French; John Morris and Philippe Salomon, who informed the chapter on photography; my regular dinner-discussion companions Charles DeGroot, Jake Lamar, John Baxter, Wolfgang Kuhlmey, Amir Al-Anbari, John Lvoff and Barry Lando; and, of course, Ann Morrison, who inspires every word I write and edits most of them. None of these generous souls bears any responsibility for the lapses of fact and judgment herein. If this edition incites new waves of anger and derision, I must face them alone.

II.

So what did I write in *Time* that prompted such an outpouring of bile, defensiveness, and, among a few kind readers, grudging thanks?

I began by mentioning the 2007 cultural *rentrée*, the annual rush-to-market of literary and artistic products carefully timed to follow France's brain-dead summer vacation season and to precede the late-fall flurry of cultural awards. That year's harvest was especially bountiful: 727 new novels, up from 683 the previous year; hundreds of new music albums

The Death of French Culture

and dozens of new films; blockbuster art exhibitions at all the big museums; fresh programs of concerts, operas, and plays in the elegant *salles* that grace French cities. Autumn means many things in many countries, but in France it signals the dawn of a new cultural year.

And nobody, I said, takes culture more seriously than the French. They subsidize it generously; they cosset it with quotas and tax breaks. French media give it vast amounts of airtime and column inches. Every French town of any size has its annual opera or theater festival, its Maison de la Culture and, in its churches, weekend organ and chamber-music recitals.

There is one problem. All of these mighty oaks being felled in France's cultural forest make barely a sound in the wider world. Once admired for the dominating excellence of its writers, artists, and musicians, France today is a wilting power in the global cultural marketplace. That is an especially sensitive issue right now, as a forceful President sets out to restore French standing in the world. When it comes to culture, Nicolas Sarkozy has his work cut out for him.

Only a handful of the season's new novels will find a publisher outside France – and hardly any in the U.S. or the U.K., though much of the fiction sold in France is translated from the English. Earlier generations of French writers – from Molière, Balzac, Hugo, and Flaubert to Proust, Malraux, Sartre, and Camus – did not lack for audiences abroad. France's movie industry, the world's largest a century ago, has yet to recapture its New Wave eminence of the 1960s, when directors like Jean-Luc Godard and François Truffaut were rewriting cinematic rules. French films today tend to be amiable, low-budget trifles for the domestic market. American movies account for nearly half the tickets sold in French cinemas.

Paris, birthplace of Impressionism, Surrealism, and the other major -isms of modern art, has been supplanted by New York City, London, Berlin, and, increasingly, Beijing. French auction houses, which once dominated the public sales of contemporary art, today account for only a small fraction of this market. French contemporary artists receive less exposure at major museums and art exhibitions than their counterparts in the U.S., the U.K., and Germany.

France does have musicians of international repute, but no equivalents of such twentieth-century composing giants as Debussy, Satie, Ravel, and Poulenc. In popular music, French *chanteurs* and *chanteuses* such as Charles Trenet, Édith Piaf, and Charles Aznavour were once heard the world over. Today, Americans and Britons dominate the pop scene. Few French performers are famous outside their country. An exception is perhaps Carla Bruni, who achieved a measure of success abroad for her intimate, whispery singing style but is now better known for being Mrs. Nicolas Sarkozy.

France's diminished cultural profile would be just another interesting national crotchet – like Italy's low birthrate, or Belgium's split-personality politics – if France weren't France. This is a country where promoting cultural influence has been national policy for centuries, where controversial philoso-phers and showy museums are symbols of pride and patrio-tism. Though France may no longer be an economic power, a French diplomat told the *International Herald Tribune*, it remains a player on the global stage. "If Germany has Siemens," he said, "we have Voltaire."

Moreover, France has led the charge at international trade talks for an *exception culturelle* that empowers governments to keep foreign entertainment products out while subsidizing their own. French officials, who believe such protectionism is essential for saving cultural diversity from the Hollywood juggernaut, once condemned *Jurassic Park* as a "threat to French identity."

In addition, France has long assigned itself a *mission civilisatrice* (civilizing mission) to improve allies and colonies alike. In 2005, legislators even ordered high schools to teach "the positive role" of French colonialism. (The law was rescinded after educators and scholars howled.) France spends more of its gross domestic product on culture and recreation than any industrialized country. The Culture Ministry lavishes money not only on such high-culture mainstays as museums, opera houses, and theater festivals but also on popular culture forms such as folk dancing and pop music. Likewise, parliament in 2005 voted to designate *foie gras* as a protection-worthy part of the nation's cultural heritage. Like a certain other nation whose founding principles sprang from the eighteenth-century Enlightenment, France is not shy about its values. As Sarkozy observed in 2007, "In the United States and France, we think our ideas are destined to illuminate the world."

Yet France does not get much payoff overseas for all that money and effort. I will present specific examples later, but here is one telling measure of France's foreign cultural reputation: In a 2007 poll of 1,310 Americans for *Le Figaro* magazine, only 20 percent considered culture to be a domain in which France excels, far behind cuisine.

My article went on to discuss various reasons for the decline: the growing dominance of the English language, faults in the French education system, the suffocating role of government in French cultural life. I also outlined various ways to reverse the decline, especially by tapping the creative energy on the margins of French society. In the end, I concluded that French culture is alive and well, though insufficiently marketed and appreciated abroad, and that France is eminently capable of regaining its position as a major cultural force.

Looking back, I see several points I should have added to the article – the overseas success of some French architects and music groups, for instance. I would also have included a proviso that box office success is not the same as artistic quality, as if anyone really confuses the two. On the other hand, I would have emphasized that it is difficult to measure the influence of French culture abroad without looking at its weight in the global marketplace. Also, I would have made it clear I was not advocating the complete abolition of cultural subsidies, merely a bit less government intrusiveness in the cultural sphere.

Critics were quick to seize on such lapses, but a few respondents offered thoughtful rebuttals that went beyond mere attacks – and kept me up at night pondering rebuttals. Culture Minister Christine Albanel, interviewed in *Libéra-tion*, took issue with my assertion that, as she paraphrased it, "excessive cultural subsidies suffocate creativity." On the contrary, she wrote, "state support for culture is a great French tradition, which responds to changing conditions: the publishing industry was saved by the law against book discounting, and our cultural policy in the realm of cinema has prevented French films from being annihilated in the marketplace by their American counterparts." Unless, Madame Minister, such policies discourage French producers from making the kind of books and films the world really wants.

Didier Jacob on his blog said that the *Time* article "refers to a conception of culture that is today largely out of date." There are no more Molières or Prousts in France, he explained, just as there are no more Henry Jameses in the U.S. Yes, dear Didier, but there are Philip Roth, Cormac McCarthys, Don DeLillos, Thomas Pynchons, Joan Didions and until their recent deaths, world-beating talents like John Updike, Saul Bellow and Norman Mailer. Besides, James could be a colos-sal bore. Moreover, Jacob said, throughout the world "the very idea of a literary masterpiece disappeared during the second half of the twentieth century." Don't tell that to Jonathan Lethem, Edwige Danticat, Dave Eggers, Jonathan Safran Foer, Richard Powers, Marilynne Robinson, Jonathan Franzen, Amy Tan, and hundreds of other very serious U.S. writers. The purported death of the masterpiece has not stopped them from constant attempts to write the big book, the major literary statement, the Great American Novel.

Perhaps the most elaborate response came from Olivier Poivre d'Arvor with his "Letter to Our American Friends." After *Time* published it, his Culturesfrance expanded the missive into a booklet distributed around the world. That version also included a list of 300 "creators, French or working in France, who are famous in a minimum of 20 foreign countries each." The list was compiled by "consulting Culturesfrance associates in close to 80 countries." A wise expenditure of taxpayer money, to be sure. But was it really prudent to have included Brigitte Bardot?

Reasonable points from my worthy critics, and forcefully argued. But do they mean that I was wrong about French culture having lost its international influence? Not really, and I'll tell you why. But first, a few words on how I got into this mess in the first place.

III.

I am, in a curious way, a product of France's *mission civilisatrice*. The American Middle West in the 1950s and early '60s was a cultural wasteland, a stupefyingly isolated desert where football, church, and television (only a handful of channels in that pre-cable, pre-digital age) were the major sources of diversion. But if you had my peculiar childhood luck, there was an alternative. I was raised by nuns. I would have preferred wolves, but my parents had other ideas.

The nuns in question were Ursulines, members of the order founded in 1535 by Angela Merici of Brescia and named after the fourth-century virgin and martyr Ursula. (A Latin scholar might say I was raised by bears.) The Ursulines came to France around 1639 and thrived there, taking education of young children as their special mission. In the eighteenth and nineteenth centuries they poured into North America, setting up shop in Quebec, New York, New Orleans, and smaller outposts – among them Alton, Illinois, the forlorn town of my birth.

It was there, at age five, that I was enrolled in an Ursuline kindergarten. From that I graduated to a nearby Ursuline elementary school, and next to the town's Ursuline-run high school. I escaped to a secular university, but soon I met a young woman studying at the College of New Rochelle, a four-year institution of higher education operated by – who else? – the Ursulines. Of course I married her.

But back to school. The town of Alton is just across the Mississippi River from St. Louis, Missouri, a much bigger city that was founded by the French in 1764. St. Louis retains some of its French architecture, street names, and other traces of the region's status as a former French colony. So does Alton, also settled by the French a half-century later. I grew up reading about the exploits of seventeenth-century French explorers such as Père Jacques Marquette (after whom my high school was named) and Louis Joliet, who camped on ground over which I frolicked as a child. Other local figures of note were the Comte de Frontenac, Pierre Laclède, and Michel-Guillaume Jean de Crèvecœur, all of them key figures in the early history of America. Many of my schoolmates had French names, as did several surrounding towns.

From the very beginning, my Ursuline teachers – none of them French but a few from French-speaking Quebec – were my windows on French culture, language, and history. As a very young child I learned to sing "Frère Jacques," though for years I had no idea what the words meant. The ramshackle U.S. education system has never put a premium on studying foreign languages, and I was not given the opportunity until age fourteen. I had a choice between French and Spanish; the latter was then, as now, the most widely studied foreign tongue in the U.S. and was certainly so at my school. I, however, chose French, which the better-looking girls were studying.

My teacher was a tough old nun who had never set foot in France, but whose mania for drills and discipline helped give me a fair reading knowledge of the language (though virtually no speaking ability). French books seemed easily available then, and I cannot help but wonder what role the French government played in that bounty. I read Hugo and Balzac, Voltaire and Montesquieu, Montaigne and Flaubert, Maupassant and even Duras, whom my nuns considered shockingly racy. When I first learned of Diderot's *Encyclopédie*, I resolved to write one of my own. I never got past the letter "A." Still, I knew that Frank Sinatra's "My Way" was a rip-off of Claude François's "Comme d'habitude," and that when Bobby Darrin sang "Beyond the Sea," he was merely reprising Charles Trenet's "La mer." I did not have much time for Elvis Presley or James Dean, but I did admire the suave charm of Maurice Chevalier and Charles Boyer. I preferred things French – whether toast, cuffs, or kissing. For me, France was the zenith of thought and culture, style and sophistication.

Forgive me this biographical digression, but while I was writing it Daniel Pennac's *Chagrin d'école* was riding high atop French bestseller lists. That fragrant memoir of the author's school days reminded me how childhood experience can shape one's life. In my case, a sentimental education ignited in me a reverence for culture and a determination to get to France. Frustratingly, I was unable to attain that latter goal until my mid-twenties. Something to do with a lack of money, the Vietnam War, and my military service obligation. But finally I washed up at Calais one dawn after a vomit-splashed nighttime train-and-boat journey from London, where I had just begun graduate school. When the Calais shops opened, I was surprised to discover that people more or less understood the strange sounds I uttered, relics of half-forgotten French classes. Over the years I returned many times, the pull of France remaining strong throughout my career as a journalist. When I was finally able to stop working, more than three decades after that first landing, the New Rochelle girl and I chose to live in France full-time. For the culture, of course.

So when my former colleagues at *Time* proposed that I take up my pen once more and write a longish article on the decline of France as a cultural power, I could hardly be expected to resist. But resist I did. Being newly retired, I did not need the work. Besides, I valued my rich Parisian life of reading, dining, hanging out in museums and opera houses, traveling around the splendid countryside, and otherwise enjoying French civilization. I am hardly alone. Not only is France the No. 1 European tourist destination for Americans, but tens of thousands of us have chosen to settle here full-time. And, as I said in the magazine article, if you live here, you cannot step out the door without stumbling over evidence of the country's cultural vitality. The notion that

France was somehow lacking in that department seemed, on the face of it, absurd. But what I had not noticed was that French culture wasn't getting much traction overseas.

Michael Elliott noticed. As the New York-based editorial director of *Time*'s international editions, he was well positioned to spot inconsistencies like that. He and *Time*'s European editor, William Green, got me to agree. (It helped that the pitch was made at a French restaurant in London with a wine list deep in treasures from the Loire.) Both men are English, though they have worked all over the world. Still, one cannot help but wonder whether, given the long history of rivalry between the two countries, an Englishman might be well-disposed to find signs of decline in France that an American like me might overlook.

So I dug into the subject with enthusiasm. I was surprised at what I found.

IV.

Cultural decline is a difficult phenomenon to assess. It speaks to the nostalgia of some French for the more rigorous, hierarchical society of the nineteenth and early twentieth centuries. Rigor, of course, is in the mind of the beholder – as is the very meaning of culture. That word has its origins in growing things, agriculture. Eventually it came to embrace the cultivation of taste in art, music, poetry, and other high-culture pursuits of a high-minded élite. These were not idle pastimes. To pursue them, as Montesquieu noted, was "to render an intelligent being yet more intelligent." The nineteenth-century English poet and critic Matthew Arnold famously described culture as the "pursuit of our total perfection by means of getting to know . . . the best which has been thought and said in the world." In his view, such contact was essential for the development of a healthy democracy. This rather Platonic notion of culture assumed that characteristics like beauty and perfection exist in the abstract and are the same for all societies.

The Death of French Culture

In modern times, scholars have broadened the definition considerably. For André Malraux, "Culture is the sum of all the forms of art, of love, and of thought, which, in the course of centuries, have enabled man to be less enslaved." Lest he seem overly Platonist, the one-time Culture Minister also termed it "the combination of mysterious responses that makes one human." The standard college-textbook description of culture today, as articulated by anthropologists Daniel Bates and Fred Plog, is "the system of shared beliefs, values, customs, behaviors and artifacts that the members of society use to cope with their world and with one another, and that are transmitted from generation to generation through learning." That definition, widely accepted by scholars, embraces low-culture enthusiasms, as well as caste systems, burial customs, and other shared behavior.

Yet when one speaks of the decline of French culture, it is clear that the discussion is not so much about customs and belief systems as about art, literature, music, and other forms of expression of the high-culture sort. Educated people, especially in Europe, remain suspicious of low, or popular, culture, with its roots in entertainment, the mass media and the marketplace. Hannah Arendt, in her influential 1963 essay "The Crisis in Culture," said that works of art should be "deliberately removed from the processes of consumption and usage and isolated against the sphere of human life necessities." Like her, I believe that culture should somehow be above commerce. Yet I grudgingly accord low-culture entertainment some space in my definition, since it is just another, if less fancy, version of the classical music, art-house cinema, and museum-quality painting and sculpture whose beauty and perfection educated people are supposed to value. So let's include culture both high and low in this discussion. Indeed, the French government protects, and the French public cherishes, both kinds as essential to the identity of France.

Measuring the global influence of a country's cultural output is an inexact science. There are, as we shall see, various empirical tools available – opinion polls, reputational rankings, box-office results, bestseller lists. As previously noted, I and Americans generally have been accused of confusing cultural excellence with mere popularity. As a reader of Pierre Assouline's blog wrote with high sarcasm in response to the *Time* article: "The hot dog is infinitely superior to the blanquette of veal. That's easy to calculate. You need only look at the sales figures. Because outside the figures, nothing exists, right?"

Wrong – unless, of course, you think the Ford Focus is infinitely superior to the Mercedes SL, or Mouton Cadet to Mouton Rothschild. If such dubious assertions were remotely true, the hot dog would be more highly valued – that is, would command a higher price – than the blanquette. This is a pointless debate.

And yet, invoking metrics like the ones mentioned above does tend to convey the impression that art is a commercial enterprise, that artworks are mere commodities to be bought and sold. Clearly, that is not the case. Art is an expression of the soul, the mind, the creative impulse. It may be influenced by the social, political, and economic conditions under which it is created, but in the end art is art. As the critic Walter Benjamin put it: "One of the foremost tasks of art has always been the creation of a demand which could be fully satisfied only later."

At the same time, artists and performers do produce works that get bought and sold at prices that can be compiled and analyzed. Art is thus a bit like light, which, physicists tell us, exhibits the behavior both of waves and of particles. You can measure the impact of the particles, but you cannot deny that light also has wave-like properties which transcend mere particle-weighing. My French critics, especially those in government, are similarly of two minds about culture. They insist it is not a commodity whose worth can be measured in sales figures. At the same time, however, they seek to protect it from foreign competition and subsidize its export as if it were in fact a commodity. Indeed, French officials have boasted to me that government subventions for their country's "cultural patrimony" – all those fabled museums, chateaux, and churches – have helped make tourism a major pillar of the French economy. One bureaucrat even tried to persuade me that a major reason tourists come to France is that they have seen French movies at home. I scoffed – but later uncovered a 2004 Ifop poll that pretty much supports his assertion.[3]

What makes one work of art worth more than another is a subject of much speculation, little agreement. Yet such differences exist. Large paintings generally command higher prices than small ones, all other things being equal. Contemporary works by German artists tend to fetch more than those by their French counterparts, for some reason. Does that mean that miniatures and French artists are not "good"? Hardly. At the same time, art critics, historians, and other experts will often form a consensus about the quality of a given work or body of work. Meanwhile, the dealers and collectors who make up the international art market may come up with a very different opinion about the same stuff. So you can have relative excellence determined either by élite critics or by crass consumers and merchants. And if you maintain that the experts are definitely the more reliable, more appropriate judges, you'll risk being accused of élitism – of endorsing a value system in which the privileged classes are the arbiters of excellence.

And they are often wrong. Edouard Manet, now recognized as one of the giants of nineteenth-century French art, was during his lifetime considered inferior to the then-celebrated Ernest Meissonier, who is little known today. When Manet died in 1883, the entire contents of his studio was sold for about the going price of a large Meissonier. Marcel Duchamp, father of the Dada movement and a believer in upending conventional notions, famously suggested a standard of utility for assessing art: "Use a Rembrandt as an ironing board."

The idea of applying empirical measurements to culture reminds me of those nineteenth-century pseudo-scientists who tried to ascertain the mass of the soul by weighing a human body just before and again just after death, and subtracting the latter from the former. These seekers of truth often came up with a number, though whether it meant anything was open to question. But how else to tell if a country's culture is faring well overseas than to measure those few things that can be measured? Otherwise, you would end up with anecdotal evidence and purely subjective observations. So you will see some numbers in the following pages. They cannot possibly tell the whole story of French culture's vitality in the world today. But at the same time, they are instructive. To ignore them would be folly.

V.

There are, in fact, two literary *rentrées* every year. In addition to the big autumn dump of new books, there is a slightly smaller one shortly after January 1. (Warning: numbers ahead.) Thus, in addition to the 659 new novels published in France in autumn 2009, another 491 appeared in winter 2010, 67 fewer than the previous year's hivernal *rentrée*. In fact, France's 10,000 publishers (according to the Syndicat National de l'Édition, an industry group) produce around 60,000 new titles of all kinds in a typical year. The numbers fluctuate only slightly from one year to the next, though the French obsesses about them. Eugène Morel, a French statistician who compiled annual totals of books published in France, did notice a gradual diminution in total output over the years. "In fact," he said, "there is an all-round decline in the French book trade, which forms a grave peril to our intellectual life and is causing us to drop far behind neighboring nations in that respect." He said this in 1911. Since then, the number of books published in France has risen steadily.

Of course, the press and the public take seriously only the thousand or so new novels that appear in the two *rentrées*, plus a similar number of mostly nonfiction books that dribble out in between. Altogether they form what can be considered the core of contemporary French literature. Within France, it is read widely and fussed over on TV talk shows, in literary magazines, and at dinner parties. Outside France, it is widely ignored.

Only a small fraction of those new novels ever get published beyond France. Fewer than a dozen appear in the U.S. or the U.K. in a given year. More precisely, the Center for Book Culture put the annual number of French novels published in the U.S. at 8.7 for the period 2000–2006. The Dalkey Archive Press, a respected U.S. publisher of translated works that takes its name from Irish writer Flann O'Brien's 1964 novel *The Dalkey Archive*, figured it at 8.5 for 2000–2005. True, that was more titles than the U.S. took during the same period from Italian authors (6.5) or Germans (6.0), but it is hardly anything to brag about. (The U.K. is thought to import roughly the same numbers of French, Italian and German titles per year as the U.S. does.)

France fares considerably better in the non-English speaking world, especially among European neighbors. In Germany, for instance, 9.4 percent of translated literary titles published in 2005 were from the French, more than any language except English – but still a very distant second: English was the original language for about 60 percent of translated novels in Germany. The numbers, which vary slightly every year, are similar in Italy and Spain: there, as in most of Europe, French literature takes second place to English. In a 2009 list compiled by the French magazine *Livres Hebdo*, six of Europe's top ten best-selling authors were British. Only one, Muriel Barbery (*The Elegance of the Hedgehog*), was French.

By some measures, French literature is holding its own in the world. The Syndicat National de l'Édition reported that foreign-language rights to 2,026 French works were sold in 2006. The biggest markets were Italy (187 titles), Spain (153) and Russia (133). At the same time, France bought translation rights to 433 foreign novels. Thus, France was a net exporter of literature, selling the rights to 4.7 titles for every one it bought. But France's performance in the important English-speaking market was far less impressive. French publishers bought the rights to 240 English-language books in

2004 but sold only 90 French titles to the Anglo-Saxons (split evenly between the U.S. and the U.K.). So France maintains a literary trade deficit with the Anglophone world. PEN, the international writers' organization, estimates that about 30 percent of works in translation sold in the U.S. were originally in French. That sounds impressive, except that most of those titles are by familiar names from the past: Gide, Malraux, Sartre, Camus, Duras, Sagan. Living authors are not high on the list. So French literature does just fine in the U.S. and the U.K., except for the kind being written today.

One group of French authors seem to have a prominence that outweighs their sales. They are known widely – though not in their home country – as the French theorists. These include Jacques Lacan (psychoanalysis), Claude Lévi-Strauss (anthropology), Roland Barthes (semiotics), Michel Foucault (philosophy and history), Gilles Deleuze and Félix Guattari (philosophy and psychoanalysis), Jean-François Lyotard (philosophy and literary theory), Jacques Derrida, Pierre Bourdieu and Jean Baudrillard (social and cultural theory), as well as several others. They do not comprise a movement so much as an eagerness to look at the world in a different way. Some, like Derrida, have sought to "deconstruct" it – sometimes from a leftist, Marxist, or otherwise radical point of view – by pursuing the meaning of a text so rigorously that it is shown to have several, often contradictory meanings. Others, such as Bourdieu, followed a more down-to-earth course, mixing theory with observations of actual human behavior (and, in Bourdieu's case, becoming involved in the real-life debates that marked French politics from the 1960s almost until his death in 2002). Whatever their approach, the French theorists brought new energy to their fields and gained a wide following, especially in the 1960s, in France and elsewhere. Their influence faded at home in the mid-'70s with the rise of the anti-Marxist, less radical "civic humanism" of the so-called *nouveaux philosophes*.

Yet the French theorists found a new audience at American universities, especially in literature departments, and they inspired successive waves of deconstructionists, anti-deconstructionists, post-deconstructionists, and anti-post-deconstructionists – as well as some very good all-round scholars. French theory, admitted Baudrillard in a 2005 interview, "was the gift of the French. They gave Americans a language they did not need. It was like the Statue of Liberty. Nobody needs French theory."[4]

But the Americans ate it up. While academic jargon rarely penetrates everyday conversation in the U.S., Americans are familiar enough with these French imports that Woody Allen could call a 1997 movie *Deconstructing Harry*. The title had to be changed for the French market (to *Harry dans tous ses états*). Apparently, not enough French moviegoers would have known what "deconstructing" means.

Today, French theory seems to be in decline. Outside a few U.S. university English departments, its die-hard adherents form an embattled minority in academic circles. The problem is not so much that the ideas have been discredited. Baudrillard was cranking out canny observations on the power of media and images up to his death in 2007, and Bourdieu's concepts of social and cultural capital, and how people negotiate the social networks they inhabit, remain widely discussed. No, the problem is that France is not producing many new Baudrillards and Bourdieus. Only a handful of living French thinkers have global reputations: Julia Kristeva, André Comte-Sponville, and the (no longer so new) *nouveaux philosophes* André Glucksmann, Alain Finkielkraut, and Bernard-Henri Lévy. BHL's 1977 *Barbarism with a Human Face* and his 2003 *Who Killed Daniel Pearl?* were international sensations. But French philosophers have generally been overshadowed by Anglo-Saxon counterparts such as John Rawls, Robert Nozick, Nicholas Sturgeon, and Richard Boyd, and by Germany's Jürgen Habermas. American, British, and German universities are where the world's great historians, sociologists, psychologists, and other thinkers congregate – France's among them. Loïc Wacquant, for instance, one of the most original of the younger French theorists and, in a sense, Bourdieu's heir in the field of sociology, teaches at the University of California at Berkeley. "The weakness of the French intellectual presence internationally troubles me," said Paul Holdengraber, director of programs at the New York Public Library, during a 2009 Festival of New French Writing in New York City organized by Culturesfrance. "It's always the same authors who get invited. Who are the new 'new philosophers'?"

Indeed, there is evidence that French writers and thinkers across the spectrum have lost their impact in the world. The *Times Literary Supplement*'s 1995 list of the most influential books of all time has a respectable thirteen French entries, but they taper off as the decades go by: five books on the list are from the 1940s, four from the 1950s, three from the 1960s, and only one from the 1970s and beyond (Raymond Aron's 1983 *Mémoires*). When America's *Foreign Policy* and Britain's *Prospect* magazines in 2005 collaborated in asking readers to vote for the world's 100 most influential "public intellectuals," more than 20,000 people from around the globe responded. The U.S. had thirty-one names on the final list, Britain twelve, China five, Germany, Canada, and India three each. France had two (Baudrillard and Finkielkraut), the same as Italy, Japan, Kenya and Switzerland. A 1997 list by members of the International Sociological Assocation of the ten most influential books in their field included only one by a French writer, Bourdieu's *Distinction: A Social Critique of the Judgment of Taste.* Said Jean Baudrillard in his 2005 interview: "There are no more French intellectuals. What you call French intellectuals have been destroyed by the media. They talk on television, they talk to the press and they are no longer talking among themselves . . . We don't pay attention to what comes from outside. We accept only what we invented."

If France gave the U.S. a handful of theorists, America has given France about one-third of all the foreign writers who are read in the Hexagon. Specifically, the proportion of new novels published in France that have been translated from a foreign language has varied from 30 percent to 40 percent over the past decade (40.3 percent in 2007). Almost three-quarters of the 3,441 translated books published in 2007 were originally in English. And, according to the Syndicat National de l'Édition again, in 2006 almost half of the English novels to which French publishers bought the rights were American. In other words, the U.S. accounts for one-third of all foreign translations sold in France.

Foreign fiction – especially the topical, realistic, plot-heavy kind favored by British and American authors – does particularly well in France. Such story-driven Anglo-Saxons as John le Carré, Pat Conroy, Ian McEwan, Graham Swift, James Ellroy and William Boyd are over-represented on French bestseller lists. Meanwhile, authors such as Diane Johnson, Nancy Huston, Jake Lamar, Douglas Kennedy and Paul Auster are treated virtually as adopted sons. Auster, who lived in France for several years translating French literature into English, is especially valued for his suspenseful, nouveau-roman influenced fiction. Indeed, his novel *The Brooklyn Follies* appeared in France more than a year before its 2006 U.S. publication. Douglas Kennedy has also lived in France and is fluent in its language, though he writes in English. His novels are instant bestsellers in France but rarely appeared in the U.S. until 2010. As the American novelist Jim Shepard (*Love and Hydrogen*) said during a 2004 visit to Paris, "Hardly anyone knows I write in my [Massachusetts] hometown. Here I walk down the street and a guy flags me down and says, 'Hey, aren't you Jim Shepard? I love your books!'"[5]

The appetite for foreign writing may help explain the astonishing success in 2006 of *Les Bienveillantes* (The Kindly Ones), a 900-page paving stone of a novel. The book had sold some 700,000 copies by the end of 2007 and won both the Prix Goncourt and the Prix de l'Académie Française. The author, Jonathan Littell, an American raised in France, wrote the book in French, though few critics praised his language skills. More important to the novel's success was its ambition, erudition, emotional power, and graphic description. In a rare interview with *Le Monde*, Littell suggested that the book may have satisfied "a demand for bigger, more fantastic, very constructed novels." That, commented American critic Elisabeth Vincentelli, is "exactly what many say contemporary French novelists are unable to provide, a common complaint being that nobody in France knows how to write large-scale stories anymore."[6]

The importance of the English-language market for the influence of French literature in the world cannot be overemphasized. English is the first language of an estimated 400 million people, more than any tongue but Chinese. Welsh eco-linguist David Crystal estimates that another 400 million speak English as a second language, and uncounted millions more have some reading knowledge of it.[7] The British Council found a decade ago that 27 percent of the world's books are published in English (compared to 12 percent in German and 8 percent in French). A survey by the French magazine *Livres Hebdo* found that 13 of Europe's 40 best-selling novels of 2008–09 were originally written in English (versus 5 in French).

But the real importance of English is that it has become a transmission belt for getting a country's literature to the rest of the world. Typically, a book is translated first into English, and that version – not the original – attracts the attention of publishers elsewhere. "A work translated into English does not merely reach an audience of native-speakers – it reaches a global audience," writes Esther Allen, director of the Center for Literary Translation at Columbia University in a study on the issue for PEN, the international writers' organization.[8] "And even without such subsequent translations, a work originally written in or translated into English will have access to the largest book market on the globe and can be read by more people of different linguistic backgrounds, nationalities and cultures than a work in any other language. English is the world's strongest literary currency."

Nonetheless, France works hard to increase the value of its own currency. The Ministry of Culture spends about 10 million euros a year on the development and export of French publications and the sale of rights to foreign publishers. The

The Death of French Culture

Ministry's Centre National du Livre (CNL) puts up 20 to 50 percent of translation costs for about 500 French titles a year. The Ministry of Foreign Affairs' Publishing Aid Program (PAP) supports books of cultural importance. In the U.S., for example, the PAP's Hemingway Grant pays one to six thousand dollars to a U.S. publisher of a French book to defray the cost of translation.

It is not just the government that supports homegrown literature. France takes its writers seriously. More than 900 literary prizes are on offer – a number few countries can match – and the big awards are front-page news every year. When Jacques Derrida died in 2004, his picture was splashed across the covers of the major newspapers, his career eulogized by the President and the Prime Minister. It was much the same a month earlier, at the death of Françoise Sagan, who had not written much of significance in decades. And yet, *Le Figaro* said, her loss "leaves France in despair."

Not many countries have equivalents of the Académie Française and the Institut de France, which make important contributions to the nation's linguistic and literary heritage. Few countries have so many television programs on writers and poets (one such show, *Apostrophes*, was for years the most-watched 90 minutes in France). No country has the equivalent of *Lire*, a popular magazine about books that has a circulation of nearly 90,000 – let alone a similar magazine, *Books*, with a somewhat smaller readership. In France, even fashion magazines carry serious book reviews, and authors are occasionally featured in fashion spreads. A 2009 survey for *Le Figaro Littéraire* found that 29 percent of French intend to write a book someday – and 3 percent already have. Perhaps not surprisingly, France claims a dozen Nobel literature laureates, more than any other country. France loves its writers. The problem is French literature itself, which has become esoteric, detached from the real world, and maddeningly difficult to export.

The French did not invent the novel, but they certainly dominated that form in the nineteenth century and into the twentieth: Stendhal, Balzac, Hugo, Dumas *père et fils*, Flaubert, Zola, Proust, Céline ... French novelists back then did not have trouble finding an international audience. Hugo's 1862 *Les Misérables* was perhaps the first international publishing "event," hitting booksellers simultaneously in Amsterdam, London, Paris, and New York. Altogether, 7 million copies were sold during the nineteenth century, earning Hugo more money than any writer had made before. Zola's *La Terre* (The Earth) was published in Paris in 1887 and in London the following year. Balzac and Dumas were bestselling authors in the U.S. Friedrich Engels, living in London, said he preferred Balzac to Zola, but read them both. Of the 30 novels serialized in the press of Transylvania in the 1890s, most were French. In the world of fiction, France was the center of attention.

Things started to go off the rails in the mid-twentieth century with the appearance of the *nouveau roman*, a kind of antinovel that jettisons conventional components of fiction such as verisimilitude and plot in favor of heady, sometimes confusing experimentation. This development was abetted by the rise of structuralism, a sprawling intellectual movement that argues, among other things, that human behavior is determined not so much by free will as by various "structures" such as kinship or class. Structuralist literary thought grew out of linguistics and holds that the novelty value of a literary text lies in new structure, not in the specifics of character development and voice. An elegant and provocative theory, but it makes for difficult novels.

Early practitioners of the *nouveau roman* included Nathalie Sarraute, Claude Simon, Alain Robbe-Grillet, and Michel Butor. Today not many writers would claim the *nouveau roman* mantle, but its influence persists in subtle ways. Contemporary French novels can be confusingly experimental, self-occupied, claustrophobic, and, as the French despairingly call them, *nombriliste* (navel-gazing). Complains the *Independent*'s John Lichfield: "French fiction writing is still mostly stuck in over-intellectualized, self-absorbed abstraction rather than story-telling."[9]

The Death of French Culture

Unlike the socially conscious novelists of the nineteenth century, the politically engaged writers of the pre- and post-World War II eras, or the idealistic generation of 1968, French writers today have largely shunned the real world of politics, globalization, poverty, terrorism, ecological peril, financial crisis, and other pressing concerns, and instead retreated into a realm of intimacy and anecdote. "Lazy prose, easy narcissism and a peculiar brand of knee-jerk pessimism," was how one U.S. critic summed up the fall 2004 literary *rentrée*.[10]

In her 2004 book *Professors of Despair*, Paris-based Canadian author Nancy Huston denounced European and especially French writers for wallowing in a "sterile nihilism" and treating optimism with contempt. Huston was especially hard on Michel Houellebecq, one of France's few contemporary writers widely published abroad, whose taste for misogyny, misanthropy, and meandering narrative has made him the poster boy for difficult French fiction (heavy helpings of sex boost his sales). An easy target perhaps. Other French authors with international reputations are eminently readable. Consider Anna Gavalda, whose 2004 novel *Hunting and Gathering* was translated into 38 languages and turned into a film (directed by Claude Berri). Still, her books, like many French novels, tend to be intimate accounts of personal relationships.

Especially annoying to critics like Huston is the rise of "autofiction," a kind of romanticized autobiography that, while occasionally absorbing, can also be shamelessly self-indulgent. The term was invented in 1977 by novelist Serge Doubrovsky, who defined it as "fiction of events and facts that are strictly real." It has since strayed from reality, and the term has become something of a pejorative. As such, it is rarely pinned on specific authors. Catherine Millet's scandalously frank 2001 memoir *The Sexual Life of Catherine M.* could probably be included, as could Christine Angot's 1999 *L'inceste*, which describes a sexual relationship with her father that may or may not have taken place. Angot received the 2006 Prix de Flore for *Rendez-vous*, an exhaustively introspective dissection of her (alleged) love affairs. Sometimes it seems that half the novels published in France are mostly about their authors.

"Autofiction is a huge problem in France," *Lire* editorial director François Busnel told me in 2007 amid the clutter of his book-piled Paris office. "I'd say 70 percent of the *rentrée* books this year are autofiction memoirs. If literature is not about my own problems, it's very hard – all the research, the development of universal characters. But if I have an affair, I take the Métro, I break up, and I can write about it all, it's much easier. The rise of structuralism and the *nouveau roman* meant that literature became a kind of therapy. Now everybody thinks he can write." That lament was echoed by Anne Carrière, director of the publishing house Éditions Anne Carrière. "The first advice I like to give young authors is 'stop confiding your miseries to the pen,'" she wrote in *Lire* in April 2007. "Three-quarters of the manuscripts I receive are psychotherapy sessions, not novels. And frankly, your little personal problems interest no one."

Perhaps that is why so few French novels interest anyone outside France, especially in the English-speaking world. Even Jean Baudrillard has said he prefers American fiction to French. Not a single French work made the *New York Times* list of the 100 "notable" books of 2008, or a *Financial Times* list of 28 important novels for 2008 – or even *Time*'s 2007 list of the best 100 novels since the magazine's 1923 founding. A French writer has not won America's fifty-thousand-dollar Neustadt International Prize for Literature in translation since Francis Ponge in 1974, though the 1996 winner, Algeria's Assia Djebar, writes in French.

The problem may be the inability of French fiction, unlike its Anglo-Saxon counterpart, to deal with the real world. "This is a country where literature is still taken seriously," Douglas Kennedy, whose 2007 novel about, among other things, the French immigrant experience, *The Woman in the Fifth,* was a bestseller in France, told me over lunch in Paris. "But if you look at American fiction, it deals with the American condition one way or another. French novelists produce interesting stuff, but what they are not doing is looking at France."

Such critiques were thrown in my face in October 2008, when Jean-Marie Gustave Le Clézio was awarded the Nobel Prize for literature. How could I accuse French writing of being dead – or even in decline, or out of touch, or incapable of appealing to a global audience – when a French author had just won the literary world's greatest gong? Or so I was asked by numerous interviewers. (I ran into Le Clézio in a Paris radio studio the morning the prize was announced. He seemed stunned by all the attention. Later that day he was asked about my *Time* article. "Some people are speaking of the decline of French culture," he replied. "I deny it. It's a very rich, very diversified culture, so there is no risk of decline.")

But as I told my journalistic inquisitors in the weeks that followed, one prize going to one author does not transform all of French literature overnight. Moreover, Le Clézio is not a typical French writer. He grew up in Mauritius and Nigeria, and he has lived outside France for most of his life. Despite an early flirtation with the *nouveau roman*, his writings are remarkably un-French, in the sense that they have exotic foreign settings and themes that are both global and topical: environmental degradation, the plight of the immigrant, globalization's human toll. He is not exactly your self-referential, navel-contemplating autofictioneer. Horace Engdahl, then permanent secretary of the Swedish Academy, acknowledged Le Clézio's uniqueness shortly after the award was announced. "He is not a typical Frenchman," Engdahl said approvingly. "He is a nomadic writer. He doesn't belong anywhere."

Interestingly, Le Clézio was among 44 leading literary figures who signed the 2007 "Manifesto for a 'World Literature' in French." That document called for French writers to abandon the arid formalism of the *nouveau roman* and instead engage the world more directly, with the goal of transforming French literature from a largely domestic enterprise into a world literature written in French. The manifesto also insisted that France's literary establishment stop looking down its nose at "francophone" authors, as foreigners writing in French are known, because those very novelists – many from former French colonies – hold the key to energizing French literature.

A pity that more French authors do not embrace that proposition. Instead, they are content, by and large, to be very French – and read chiefly in France. "There is a downside to the relatively high status of writers in this country," says *Lire*'s François Busnel. "In America, writers want to work hard and be successful. They're not interested in going to parties. They don't have a Café Flore to gather in. But French writers think they have to be intellectuals." French critics encourage that view. They tend to praise the more difficult novels and dismiss the more accessible ones. Take the simple, emotionally satisfying works of Marc Lévy, who moved 1.7 million copies in 2009 – the sixth year in a row that he was France's best-selling author.[11] (He published two novels that year, *Le Premier jour* and *La Première nuit*.) Yet even though his books have sold more than 20 million copies in 41 countries, Lévy has won hardly any critical acclaim in his home country. Perhaps not surprisingly, he moved to London a few years ago. Says cultural commentator Frédéric Martel: "Nearly every book that is famous in France became a success without the help of the critics."

Publishers are more than willing to perpetuate this system. Under the *prix unique du livre*, a law introduced in 1981, it is illegal to sell a new book in France for less than 95 percent of its list price. So publishers can make money on fewer copies of a title than can their counterparts in countries where discounting is allowed. Some people think there are too many books published in France. "We have 25 readers working seven days a week, and they still can't keep up," said François Busnel, describing *Lire*'s reviewing mechanism. "So maybe half of the 727 new novels this fall [2007] will get a reading. Of these only 10 or 20 will get chosen for a review, and only six or seven will have some commercial success. And yet publishers still keep going. They don't care.

The Death of French Culture

They're making money, not much, but enough." Said Jean d'Ormesson, novelist and member of the French Academy: "We can reproach French editors for publishing far too much. But at least it is true that if they publish a lot of rubbish, they don't miss a lot of works of genius."[12] Unfortunately, the world outside France cannot tell the difference.

VI.

Cinema was born in France. Léon Bouly invented the movie camera in 1892, and Auguste and Louis Lumière organized the first-ever public film screening in 1895 (at Paris's Grand Café). At the beginning of the twentieth century, France had the largest movie industry in the world, and a majority of films shown in the U.S. and the U.K. were French. But production was virtually halted during World War I, and by the time peace returned Hollywood had stolen the crown. Nonetheless, France retained considerable influence in the cinematic world. Inspired by an influx of American films in the 1920s, young French filmmakers launched an avant-garde movement that changed the way movies were made everywhere. Led by Louis Delluc, French directors perfected the use of jump cuts, soft focus, point-of-view shots and editing devices such as superimposition to create a more subjective, impressionistic experience. The surrealists and Dadaists pursued this tradition of experimentation in their own films, and France became known as the place where cinema was considered art.

That reputation was extended in the 1950s and '60s with the New Wave directors, who rejected the expensive production values of the big French studios, as well as the high-minded "cinema of quality" that dominated film festivals. Instead, the newcomers used improvisation, available light, location shooting, direct sound – and near-total directorial control, making the director the *auteur* of the film. François Truffaut, Jean-Luc Godard, Claude Chabrol, and other

French *auteurs* became cinematic heroes around the world. Since then, however, French cinema has lost much of its international clout.

In the three decades before 1970, France claimed the Academy Award for Best Foreign Film a total of eight times, more than any other country. In the three decades since then, France has taken home only one such Oscar (for *Indochine* in 1992). French films have a better record at the Cannes Film Festival – though perhaps they have a home-field advantage – winning the Palme d'Or four times in the 1950s, '60s, and '70s, and five times since then. However, two of those post-1970s winners were by directors not widely considered to be French: *Underground* by Emir Kusturica, a Serbian national, and *The Pianist* by Roman Polanski, who grew up in Poland and has rarely worked in France. Indeed, both films were shot outside the country, with non-French actors and barely a word of French dialogue. French movies have also done better at the Berlin Film Festival, winning the Golden Bear six times since the festival began in 1951. After *Alphaville* in 1965, however, France did not claim another Golden Bear for 30 years.

What happened in the 1970s and beyond? Television lured French audiences away from the cinemas, and the moviegoers who remained seemed to prefer the slick, lavishly financed films of Hollywood. According to the Centre National de la Cinématographie (CNC), U.S. films accounted for 44.5 percent of the tickets sold in France in 2008, almost as many as French movies did (45.7 percent). The two top-grossing films, *Bienvenue chez les Ch'tis* and *Astérix aux jeux olympiques*, were French, but all of the next eight were American. Increased government subsidies have kept the French film industry alive, and some foreign directors – Jane Campion, David Lynch, Wong Kar-Wai – have taken advantage of that support to make movies in France. In 2008, according to the CNC, 240 films were produced in France, more than any other country in Europe. France also has some 5,300 movie screens, the highest number in Europe and the fourth highest in the world, after China, the U.S., and India.

The Death of French Culture

But more than most countries, France protects its film industry with a blanket of subsidies and quotas. As a result, French films tend to be amiable, low-budget social comedies and other trifles made principally for the domestic market. They can barely hold their own against Hollywood imports. Though some French directors have been aiming at overseas markets, the only vaguely French film to win U.S. box-office glory in recent years was the animated *Ratatouille* – oops, that was made by Disney.

All right, *La Vie en rose*, the Édith Piaf biopic (released as *La Môme* in France), did take in 10 million dollars at the U.S. box office in 2007, making it the top-grossing foreign film of the year there. And its female lead, Marion Cotillard, won the Academy Award for Best Actress, the first French-woman to do so since Simone Signoret in 1960. But even the biggest foreign film in America is not really all that big. *La Vie en rose* would have had to earn about twice that 10 million dollars to make the year's list of 100 top-grossing films in the U.S.

In general, French movies do not fare particularly well abroad. Only about one in five gets exported to the U.S., one in three to Germany. There are only two French entries on the Internet Movie Data Base worldwide ranking of top-grossing movies of all time, and they come far down the list: director Luc Besson's 1997 *The Fifth Element*, at number 255 with 264 million dollars in sales, and his 2008 *Taken*, at number 332 with 224 million dollars. There are none on the IMDB's list of the 250 all-time box office hits in the U.S. Unifrance, the organization that promotes French movies overseas, reported that together they sold a record 84 million tickets overseas in 2008 – led by big-budget entries like *Babylon A.D.* and *Astérix aux jeux olympiques*. (Those two were among a mere seven French films that did better overseas than at home.) That was a big improvement over 2007 when, according to *Variety*, French films were seen by 57 million people outside France, down 9 percent from the year before and 32 percent from 2005.

What irks the French is that many of their movies do become hits in the U.S. – as Hollywood remakes. Thus, *Boudu sauvé des eaux* was saved again as *Down and Out in Beverly Hills*. *Le grand blond avec une chaussure noire* was re-shod as *The Man with One Red Shoe*. *Trois hommes et un couffin* was born again as *Three Men and a Baby*. *La vie continue* continued as *Men Don't Leave*. *La Cage aux folles* was uncaged in the U.S. as *The Birdcage*. *L'Appartement* was re-housed as *Wicker Park*. And so on, with new scripts, directors, and actors. Though American films sometimes get remade in France – Jacques Audiard's 2004 French hit *De battre mon coeur s'est arrêté* (The Beat that My Heart Skipped) is based on James Toback's 1978 *Fingers* – the traffic is mostly in the other direction. The world, even the Anglo-Saxon part of it, does like French movies – just not the way the French make them. Thus, it is difficult to imagine how *Bienvenue chez les Ch'tis*, at nearly 200 million euros the biggest domestic box-office success in French cinema history, could seduce a foreign audience if not through a remake: this tale of a postal worker transplanted from the south of France to the north is so thoroughly French as to defy translation. Nonetheless, Warner Brothers has bought the rights. The previous box office record-holder, 1966's *La Grande Vadrouille*, a World War II comedy starring Bourvil and Louis de Funès, has so far resisted Hollywoodization. At least some things are sacred.

France treats cinema with utmost seriousness. The country probably has more film critics, film journals, and film studies programs per capita than any place on earth. The problem is quality, or at least the perception of it. French movies, like French novels, are known for intellectual pretensions, a lack of action, and a focus on relationships instead of on social and political concerns. Sophie Marceau once described the typical French movie: "Annie sleeps with Daniel and Jérôme sleeps with Claude, then Daniel sleeps with Claude and then they discuss it all in a restaurant."[13] Even the respected

The Death of French Culture

French film magazine *Cahiers du cinéma* once concluded, with an air of despair:

> The important films of 2004 maintain a weak relationship with current affairs: scarcely any cinema is diagnosing *l'aujourd'hui*. [There] were various films that pretended to confront reality, particularly in the documentary mode. 2004 is also the year of Michael Moore [*Fahrenheit 9/11*], even though we do not recognize ourselves at all in that approach. The cinema that interests us the most forges relationships . . . constructed at a distance from reality.[14]

In recent years, that stereotype has been fading. French filmmakers have been moving toward more accessible movies that might have a chance of pleasing foreign audiences – and capturing younger French moviegoers nurtured on Hollywood films. *Le fabuleux destin d'Amélie Poulain* (Amélie) of 2001, *Les Choristes* (The Chorus) and *Un long dimanche de fiançaille* (A Very Long Engagement), both from 2004, did well commercially, though not so well with critics. Indeed, such recent French attempts at box office glory have been accused of narrative predictability, emotional manipulation, and an emphasis on production values over content. These are the sort of qualities French critics tend to dislike in Hollywood films.

Rather than ape Hollywood, France may find it more practical to pursue the kind of small- to medium-sized features – those with budgets well under 50 million dollars – that can win both cash and acclaim. In other words, movies like Hollywood's *Synechdoche New York*, *Revolutionary Road*, *Frost/Nixon*, and Britain's *The Reader*, all from 2008; or, from 2009, *The Hurt Locker*, *Julie & Julia*, *Up in the Air*, and *Precious*. In other words, France needs more films like the 27-million-dollar *La Vie en rose*: modest in scale, yet with the emotional power and simple narrative of old French cinema masterpieces.

If there is a cinematic domain in which France can still give the world lessons, it is the documentary. Witness the recent box-office success of Nicolas Philibert's *Être et avoir*

(To Be and To Have) and Luc Jacquet's *La Marche de l'empereur* (March of the Penguins). Documentaries, after all, deal with the real world, not the petty concerns of invented characters. And, as was certainly the case with the penguin movie, they can be told without the risk of talkiness. Accordingly, Laurent Cantet's *Entre les murs* (The Class), which won the 2008 Palme d'Or at Cannes and was nominated for an Oscar, suggests that France can also expand the definition of the documentary. Ostensibly a work of fiction, *Entre les murs* has certain documentary attributes (amateur actors, a real setting, the use of videotape, a story inspired by the screenwriter's life, and a subject, inner-city education, that is very much in the news). French cinema's redemption might reside within this imaginative mix of genres. Tellingly, *Entre les murs* was sold to 43 countries, even before it won the Palme d'Or.

With the internationalization of the film industry – financing coming from many countries, talent hopping back and forth to Hollywood – it is increasingly difficult to tell a movie's nationality (viz. *The Pianist*). France, with its protected domestic film market, has been largely insulated from the wider cinematic world. That idyll cannot last. Already, the big foreign films that hit France – like *Avatar* or the Harry Potter movies – play in hundreds of theaters simultaneously, leaving fewer screens for those modest, interesting productions that French critics and film buffs love. Will these small films require even more subsidies? Or can French filmmakers survive on their own in the new, more competitive world?

Some already do. Cedric Klapisch's 2003 hit *L'Auberge espagnole* (The Spanish Apartment), Mathieu Kassovitz's two *Les Rivières pourpres* (The Crimson Rivers) films and his *Babylon A.D.*, Luc Besson's *Taxi* series of Hong Kong-style action comedies and his 2008 thriller *Taken* were meant for exportation from the start, and they have proved popular among audiences at home and abroad. But not with French critics, who are notoriously hard on successful, commercial films. *L'as des as* (Ace of Aces), a lavish World War II action-comedy starring Jean-Paul Belmondo, was the biggest French

The Death of French Culture

box office hit of 1982. Yet 25 French critics issued an appeal to moviegoers to boycott the movie. They argued that *L'as des as* would crowd out smaller, more worthy films from the marketplace. It apparently did not occur to them that audiences clearly preferred the Belmondo film to the "smaller" alternatives. Or that revenue from a French-made hit might be plowed by its producers into yet more French films. "We French have a problem," Luc Besson told me and some colleagues over drinks in 2005. "We cannot admit to ourselves that movies are an industry, that a movie can also be fun." Until the French figure out how to make movies the world wants to see, they will never regain the cinematic leadership they enjoyed for decades after giving the world the gift of film.

VII.

Like French cinema and literature, French theater is steeped in history and synonymous with a roster of illustrious talent: from Corneille, Racine, and Molière to Giraudoux, Beckett, Genet, Anouilh, Ionesco, Koltès and, more recently, Denise Bonal, Michel Vinaver, and Yasmina Reza. But aside from a handful of private theaters – 155 in Paris and one in Lyons – French drama is basically an activity of the government. The state subsidizes 5 *théâtres nationaux*, 39 *centres dramatiques*, 69 *scènes nationales*, 77 *scènes conventionnées* and 600 *compagnies théâtrales* across France, all of which put on plays. These 800 or so government-funded institutions welcomed an estimated 3.8 million paying customers in the 2004–05 season, or fewer than 100 per week each. Audiences are hardly breaking down the doors to attend government-subsidized plays. Contrast that with the 3.3 million people who went to the 46 private theaters that disclose figures, an average of nearly 6,000 a week each.

Live theater is a valued part of nearly every country's cultural heritage, and France is certainly not alone in subsidizing it. But the question must be asked: Is France getting its money's worth? The Ministry of Culture announced in 2007 that it planned to look more closely at how many people patronize subsidized theaters (evidently, there are no reliable figures). The Ministry was threatening to introduce tougher criteria for evaluating subsidies and determining whether French theater is getting sufficient exposure overseas.

The answer to that last question is negative. Aside from the classics, which have long been performed in translation, French theater is rarely seen abroad. In the past four decades only two French works have won a Tony, the top American theater award, for best play (*Art* in 1994 and *The God of Carnage* in 2009, both written by Yasmina Reza). A French work has never won the Best Play prize of the New York Drama Critics' Circle in its 73-year history (though British playwright Christopher Hampton's version of Pierre Choderlos de Laclos's 1782 *Les liaisons dangereuses* took the Citation for Best Foreign Play in 1986–87). Three contemporary French works have won Best Play honors in the 54-year history of Britain's Evening Standard Theatre Awards (Jean Anouilh's *Becket* and *Poor Bitos*, and Jean Giraudoux's *The Trojan War Will Not Take Place*). A French play has never received a Laurence Olivier Award for Best New Play in Britain, though Alain Boublil and Claude-Michel Schönberg's *Martin Guerre* did win Best Musical in 1997.

Language is a factor, of course, but so is the nature of contemporary French drama. Just as its fiction was influenced adversely by the *nouveau roman*, France's drama became more abstract and difficult in the years after World War II – the era of Ionesco, Beckett, Sartre, and the theater of the absurd. Today, many French plays – especially those that debut in subsidized theaters – are intensely intellectual, sometimes claustrophobic works that do not export well.

It would perhaps be unfair to single out any recent work, but an example of a play that might not be made without government support recently caught my eye. Lyons's (government-subsidized) theater Les Ateliers condensed Jean Eustache's rambling 3 hr. 40 min. film of 1973, *La maman et la putain* (The Mother and the Whore), into a play. The

The Death of French Culture

theater's description of this work is edifying: "Alexandre is an idle young man who passes his time in the cafés of the Latin Quarter. He lives with Marie. When he tries to reclaim Gilberte, a former lover who is about to marry somebody else, he meets Veronika, a young nurse who collects sexual conquests." That sounds like a lot of contemporary French novels and movies. It would have been perfect if they had all gotten together over dinner to discuss things. I suspect the play will not make it to Broadway or the West End.

All this is not to say that French theater is dead. Local festivals, like the famous one in Avignon, abound. The success of France 2's live television broadcast of *Fugueuses*, a hit of 2007 at Paris's Théâtre des Variétés, will no doubt encourage other such telecasts. The play, written by Pierre Palmade and Christophe Duthuron and starring the durable Line Renaud and Muriel Robin, drew 8 million viewers, more than any live broadcast of a French play in memory. The experience prompted France 2 to promise more such broadcasts, though only those of reasonable length, minimal scene changes and, especially, a few big-name stars. "Without stooping to caricature, it's evident that we wouldn't put on *Le Soulier de satin* (The Satin Slipper) at 8:50 p.m.," said Patrice Duhamel, general manager of France Télévisions, referring to Paul Claudel's notoriously difficult 11-hour play of 1943.

Alas, France has focused too much energy on stupefying plays like *Le Soulier de satin* and not enough of the kind of quality, middle-market works like *Fugueuses* that abound in other countries' theaters. Plays like the New York Broadway hits *Doubt, August: Osage County,* and *Ruined,* or such recent standouts in London's West End as *Enron, Tusk Tusk,* and *Jerusalem.* Or, better yet, plays like Yasmina Reza's *God of Carnage,* a hit both on Broadway and in the West End. The play had only a brief run in France. Aside from Marc Camoletti's frothy 1965 *Boeing, Boeing* – which won a Tony in 2008 in its successful Broadway revival – France's last big hits on the world stage were probably Claude-Michel Schönberg and Alain Boublil's 1980s musicals *Les Misérables* and *Miss Saigon.* But then, French drama has long been difficult to bring to foreign audiences. "Plays are no longer mere neatly articulated dummies on which the costume of any nation can be fitted by dint of a little taking in here and letting out there," concluded the *New York Times*. "The taut and trim cats' cradle intrigue which could be slipped from the fingers of the French author to those of the English adapter, with the change of only a loop or two, is now looked upon as a bygone childish thing." The observation is from 1886.

VIII.

France was once the center of the art world. In the nineteenth and much of the twentieth centuries, the country served as the birthplace – or at least the nursery – of Fauvism, Impressionism, Post-Impressionism, Divisionism, Surrealism, Cubism, and other major artistic movements. Even the Italian Futurists chose the French daily *Le Figaro* to unveil their famous 1909 manifesto; France was where they wanted to be heard. Can any nation claim so many illustrious artistic names as could France in that glorious era? There was David, Ingres, Géricault, Delacroix, Courbet, Manet, Degas, Cézanne, Monet, Rodin, Renoir, Gaugin, Seurat, Toulouse-Lautrec, Matisse, Léger, Picasso, Braque, Duchamp, Chagall, De Staël, Klein . . .

Today, France still takes art seriously. Paris's great museums are among the world's most distinguished, certainly the most popular. Six million people a year file past the Louvre's *Mona Lisa* alone. The Centre Georges-Pompidou is a must-see for modern (that is, early- and mid-twentieth century) art, and the refurbished Palais de Tokyo is one of the most important new venues for contemporary (post-1960s) works. France also claims some of the world's best-known living artists: Louise Bourgeois, Pierre Soulages, Daniel Buren, Annette Messager, Christian Boltanski, Pierre and Gilles, Robert Combas, Pierre Huyghe, Philippe Parreno, Adel Abdessemed.

The Death of French Culture

But France's days as the powerhouse of the art world are over. Not that its artists are failing to produce interesting, head-turning work. Sophie Calle's installation in the French pavilion at the 2007 Venice Biennale, *Take Care of Yourself*, was arguably the sensation of the show. The problem is that the world is not looking. Paris has lost its leadership position in art to London, New York, and Berlin, with Beijing and Shanghai closing fast. "The U.S. now defines what world art is," says Christophe Boïcos, a Paris art lecturer and gallery owner. "In those places where contemporary art is strong, there is an economy that has more dynamism. That has been true of London since the '90s, and Berlin is coming up."

An artist's influence is an elusive beast, but the German business magazine *Capital*, which covers the global art scene intensely, came up with perhaps the best, and certainly the mostly widely accepted standard of measurement. Every year since 1970, *Capital* produced Kunst Kompass, a list of the world's 100 most influential contemporary artists. (The list was taken over by Germany's *Manager* magazine in 2008.) The ranking is based on a complicated formula that takes into account such factors as mentions in leading art publications, inclusion in major permanent collections and exposition at big international art exhibitions. For 2009, Germany had 30 names on the list, the U.S. 26 and Britain 12. France had a mere four (Boltanski, Huyghe, Buren, and Calle). No French names were in the top 20, where the U.S. had nine and Germany six.

Meanwhile, prices paid for the works of living French artists have fallen behind those of their peers in other countries. According to a 2007 survey by the art information service Artprice, *Lullaby Spring* by Britain's Damien Hirst was the most expensive work of art by an artist born after 1945 to be sold at auction that year. It went for 17 million dollars, a world record. The average Hirst work that year sold for well over a million. By comparison, the most successful French artist on the auction scene, Robert Combas, commanded about 10,000 dollars per work. That put Combas a distant No. 108 on Artprice's list of the world's 500 top-selling artists at auction (Hirst was first, of course). Other French on the list were Bernard Frize (No. 238) and Sophie Calle (No. 302). Even at home, French artists sometimes have a hard time gaining respect. Daniel Buren in 2007 threatened to destroy *Les Deux Plateaux*, the installation of striped columns in Paris's Palais-Royal that he calls "my best-known piece in the world," after the French government, which had commissioned the work, had allowed it to deteriorate.

Paris was also once the commercial capital of the art world, with galleries and auction houses that were second to none. As recently as the 1950s, France's leading auctioneer, Étienne Ader, sold twice as much art as its two big London competitors, Christie's and Sotheby's, combined. French auction houses benefited from an arcane set of rules and tax regulations that had for centuries kept outsiders from gaining a toehold in the local market. But as the global art industry grew, these barriers hindered the ability of homegrown auctioneers to raise capital and compete internationally. As a result, French houses were selling a relatively modest 1 billion dollars' worth of art a year by 1998, compared with 4.2 billion dollars for their counterparts in the U.S. and 2.4 billion dollars for those in the U.K.

Under pressure from European Union competition authorities, France began loosening the regulations in 2000, but by then it was too late. The Americans and Britons had solidified their control of the market. Auction houses in France now account for only about 8 percent of all public sales of contemporary art, calculates Alain Quemin, a sociologist at France's University of Marne-La-Vallée, compared with 50 percent for the U.S. and 30 percent for Britain. Worse, Artprice reported in 2005 that France's share of sales of all fine art, contemporary and otherwise, was a mere 6.6 percent. Christie's is now the world's largest auction house and, though bought by French billionaire François Pinault in 1998, is still based in London. (Sotheby's is a publicly traded company headquartered in the U.S.) France's position in the art market suffered another setback in late 2009 when a scandal erupted at the Hôtel Druout, the 150-year-old Paris auction house owned collectively by 70 auctioneers. According to law enforcement officials, a large number of artworks were stolen over the years by Druout staff. An auctioneer and eight porters were under formal investigation.

France was the world's third-largest art market until 2008, when it was overtaken by China. France's decline is especially evident in the market for contemporary art. That culturally indicative sector accounted for only 2.8 percent of 2007 auction sales in France, compared to 9.9 percent globally. Concluded Artprice in its 2007 annual report: "The public auction market in France is fossilising and appears to have gradually settled into a niche specialising in primitive photography, nineteenth century paintings and Art Deco." Likewise, Paris is no longer the locus of world-class art exhibitions that it was in the nineteenth century, when its Universal Expositions and Salons des Refusés changed the course of art history. Today, France's biggest entry in the art-exhibition sweepstakes, FIAC, has been overtaken in size and influence by such competitors as Switzerland's Art Basel, America's Art Basel Miami Beach, Germany's Documenta, and, soon, the Frieze Fair in London. Though France's museums remain strong, the country suffered a blow to its prestige in 2006 when François Pinault, exasperated by bureaucratic foot-dragging, decided against locating his vast art collection on the Ile Seguin just outside Paris and instead installed it in Venice. When France's major art collectors avoid their own country in favor of a neighbor, it is a sign that French culture needs help.

IX.

There is one art form that can be described, quite literally, as France's gift to the world. In 1826, scientist Joseph Nicéphore Niépce inserted a bitumen-coated plate into a box with a lens. He then pointed the contraption toward a window at his estate near Chalon-sur-Saône in southern

Burgundy. The resulting image, *View from the Window at Le Gras*,[15] is the earliest known photograph. The following year Niépce began sharing his findings with Jacques Daguerre, a Paris artist and theatrical designer. Niépce died soon after, but in 1837 Daguerre unveiled a simple, reliable way to fix images on a light-sensitive plate. Daguerre assigned the rights to his process to the French government, which in turn donated it – and the art of photography – to humankind.

The daguerreotype and its successors ignited a global frenzy of picture-taking, and France became the epicenter of the new art. Such French practitioners as Édouard-Denis Baldus, Nadar, Maxime du Camp, Auguste Salzmann, Félix Bonfils, and Eugène Atget shaped the art's development for more than a century. French photographers influenced painters Camille Corot and Jean François Millet, who collected photos to help them depict nature. Degas took up the camera himself. Man Ray and other Surrealists treasured Atget's artfully composed Parisian street scenes and were, many of them, photographers themselves. Étienne-Jules Marey's stop-action photos of human and animal movement helped inspire the Italian Futurists' attempts to depict speed. The influence worked both ways: Gustave Le Gray and Henry Le Secq produced evocative photo landscapes that resemble the oil-on-canvas scenes of Millet and other Barbizon painters. France also pioneered nude photography, inspiring not just racy postcards but also generations of more serious painting.

By the 1920s, France's photographic leadership was widely recognized. In the introductory notes to "Paris capitale photographique 1920–1940," a 2009 exhibit at Paris's Hôtel de Sully, the curators wrote: "From the beginning of the 1920s, Paris secured its place as the center of the avant garde and the new art of photography in Europe. The French capital became the crucible of encounter and exchange for photographers of diverse nationalities and horizons. That was because Paris represented a model of economic modernity and optimism just after the First World War. But it is also because the city opened its arms to numerous emigrants and

The Death of French Culture

became a place of refuge for political and confessional exiles."
Among those emigrants: Ilse Bing from Germany, Brassaï of
Hungary, and Moï Ver from Lithuania.

France's dominance continued into mid-century, a period
when the immediacy and narrative flair of such Paris-based
innovators as André Kertész, Henri Cartier-Bresson, and
Édouard Boubat influenced the emerging field of photojour-
nalism. After World War II Cartier-Bresson co-founded
Magnum, the first major cooperative photo agency. It succeeded in winning for photographers the permanent rights to
their work, which had previously gone to the assigning publications. The agency was soon joined in Paris by the re-
launched Rapho (Raymond Grosset, Willy Ronis, Robert
Doisneau), as well as by Gamma (Hubert Henrotte, Raymond
Depardon), Sygma, Sipa, Vu and others. Their appearance,
and the rise of picture-heavy international magazines like
Life and *Paris Match*, made Paris the world capital of pho-
tojournalism. France extended its photographic reputation
with the establishment of the Rencontres d'Arles Photo-
graphie in 1969, the Visa Pour l'Image festival in Perpignan
in 1989, and Paris Photo in 1997.

That silvered age has begun to fade in recent years. Picture
magazines have all but disappeared, and many of the big
Paris photo agencies have folded or merged with U.S. rivals.
As the agencies vanished, and digital technology made it
possible for their replacements to operate almost anywhere,
international news organizations found they no longer needed
a photo presence in Paris. I had the painful duty of closing
Time's Paris photo desk in 2001. The entire Paris bureau was
shuttered in 2009.

Photography itself was changing as well. The arrival on
the U.S. scene of Swiss-born Robert Frank in the 1950s
launched a new interest in street photography. Diane Arbus,
Garry Winogrand, Ed Ruscha, Joel Meyerowitz and other
Americans captured the raw excitement of urban life – much
as Atget had a half-century earlier in France, though his influence was no longer strongly felt in his homeland. The action

had moved to that dream city of gritty reality, New York. In addition, American photographers were quick to exploit the possibilities of color photography, long dismissed by serious practitioners elsewhere as eye-candy for amateur snappers. Today the world's most highly valued photographers – Jeff Wall, Andreas Gursky, Martin Parr, Richard Prince – shoot mostly in color, and not in France.

Only a single French photographer based in France made *American Photo* magazine's 2005 list of the 100 most important people in photography: Alexandra Boulat, who died in 2007. Three other French citizens were listed – fashion photographer Patrick Demarchelier, photojournalist Giles Peress and photo-retoucher Pascal Dangin – but all of them had left France years ago for the U.S.

The global art market for photographs is growing: between 1990 and 2007, according to Artprice, auction prices for photography rose 70 percent, compared to 43 percent for sculpture and 15 percent for painting. (Prices of many artworks sank during the subsequent recession, but some dealers say photography held up relatively well.) As with the rest of the art market, however, the business has shifted to New York and London, which have 65 percent and 19 percent, respectively, of worldwide photography sales at auction, versus 9 percent for Paris. The average auction price for a photograph taken by an American is around seven times that of one taken by a French photographer. Though France has many talented shooters (Carlos Freire, Stéphane Couturier, Valérie Belin, Philippe Gronon, Matthias Olmeta), they remain largely unknown outside the Hexagon. And none has come close to commanding the prices attained by German-born Andreas Gursky (whose *99 Cent II* set a photographic record at 2.27 million euros in 2006), or Americans Jeff Wall, Richard Prince, and Cindy Sherman.

France's love affair with the photograph has long been tinged with ambiguity. Photography, after all, straddles the realms of art and commerce, journalism and technology. Unlike painting, music, storytelling, and dance, it did not spring naturally, thousands of years ago, from our primal urge for self-expression. It was invented by tinkerers during the Industrial Revolution and carries with it all the French ambivalence about progress and commercialization. Moreover, photography is a technology that has become numbingly foolproof, so that just about anybody can, with minimal skills, take a decent picture. The serendipitous and thoroughly democratic nature of photography unsettles critics and élitists who believe that art should have a more direct relationship to talent. Thus, Baudelaire could only express his worry about the new art form in *Le Salon de 1859*, his essay on that year's Paris exhibition: "By invading the territories of art, [photography] has become art's most mortal enemy ... If photography is allowed to supplement art in some of its functions, it will soon have supplanted or corrupted it altogether, thanks to the stupidity of the multitude which is its natural ally." Contemporary American critic Susie Linfield put the dilemma neatly: "Where such egalitarianism dwells, can the razing of all distinctions be far behind? Who can admire an activity – much less an art – that so many people can do so damn well? Photography's democratic promise has always been photography's populist threat."[16]

France today is a photography backwater, preoccupied with the glory of its rich history. France's fine and numerous museums are filled with retrospectives of photographers long dead, its auction houses focused on selling those precious, sepia-tinged relics from a bygone age. But where are France's Jeff Walls, Richard Princes, Cindy Shermans, and Andreas Gurskys? In New York, many of them. Young French photographers of talent and reputation who do live or work in France can be forgiven if they feel underappreciated.

Helmut Newton, the provocative, enormously successful fashion photographer, lived in Paris for two decades before moving to Monaco. He did much of his work in France and once said he was particularly influenced by an iconic Brassaï photo titled *Paris by Night*. Shortly before his death in 2004, Newton offered 50 of his photographs to the French state – an amazing gift, since Newton's works are pricey and even the government often cannot outbid private collectors. The offer was met with indifference, he complained. After the Ministry of Culture declined his request to display the photos at the 2004 re-opening of the Jeu de Paume exhibition space in Paris, Newton gave them – and 1,000 others – to the city of Berlin, his birthplace, which dedicated a museum in his honor. Newton was no doubt a victim of his financial success, as well as his specialization in nude and fashion photography, long considered vulgar by French aesthetes. Newton declared to *Le Monde*: "French museums and the contemporary art world misunderstand me." Baudelaire would be pleased. France should be worried.

X.

One exception to France's artistic decline is the realm of architecture. From the invention of the Gothic in the twelfth century, through the rise of the École des Beaux Arts in the nineteenth, to the twentieth-century "international style" of Le Corbusier, France has long been a force in the design of buildings. Illustrious French practitioners have included François Mansart, Louis Le Vau, the Marquis de Vauban, Jules Hardouin-Mansart, Victor Baltard, Charles Garnier, Hector Guimard, Robert Mallet-Stevens, and dozens more. Today, France can still claim a number of internationally famous architects: Roger Taillibert (Montreal Olympic Stadium), Paul Andreu (Beijing Opera House), Bernard Tschumi (New York City's Blue Tower), Christian de Portzamparc, who is known for La Villette-Cité de la Musique and was the first French architect to win the hundred-thousand-dollar Pritzker Prize, as well as Jean Nouvel, another Pritzker laureate, who designed Paris's Institut du Monde Arabe and Musée du Quai Branly.

French architects have long benefited from the historic enthusiasm of their political leaders for *grands projets* such as François Mitterrand's Grande Bibliothèque, Opéra Bastille, and Grand Louvre, as well as Jacques Chirac's Musée du Quai Branly. Even Sarkozy has begun planning a new French history museum for Paris, though political and budgetary constraints derailed his plans for an ambitious urban renewal scheme he called "Le Grand Paris." Such presidential preference for trophy buildings has done little to improve the overall vitality and livability of France's urban areas. An example is the destruction of Baltard's graceful nineteenth-century iron pavilions at Paris's Les Halles food market and their replacement – under then-mayor Jacques Chirac – with a monstrous, 1970s-ugly warren of underground shopping arcades that became a magnet for drug dealers.

Responding to public disgust with that eyesore, the city held a competition in 2004 for a new Les Halles. Four designs – two by Dutch architects, Rem Koolhass and Winy Maas, and two by Frenchmen, Jean Nouvel and David Mangin – were selected as finalists. Parisians were invited to vote for their favorite, though the ballot was not binding. In the end, the city chose perhaps the least imaginative of the contenders, by France's Mangin. With Mayor Bertrand Delanoë approaching municipal elections and already under fire for proposing skyscrapers on the outskirts of Paris, his administration compounded its lack of nerve by declaring that Mangin's design would be used only as a master plan for the development. A new competition was called to select a design for the forum itself. The winner of that was another French team, Patrick Berger and Jacques Anziutti, with a yellowish translucent dome that left many critics and ordinary Parisians cold. When it comes to *grands projets*, France tends to favor home-grown architects, to ignore the preferences and convenience of its residents and, increasingly, to avoid choosing anything remarkable. Thus, to fulfill their most audacious projects, French architects are condemned to exile: Jean Nouvel probably couldn't have built his imaginative Agbar Barcelona tower in Paris. It isn't mediocre enough.

No one is calling Nouvel and Portzamparc mediocre, but they are part of a new group of star architects – along with non-French standouts like Frank Gehry, Richard Rogers, Norman Foster, Renzo Piano, Tadao Ando, and Zaha Hadid

– whose rise may not be an entirely welcome development for either architecture or France. With their public relations staffs and signature stylistic flourishes, they tend to dominate international competitions. Equally talented but less flamboyant architects are not pleased at this development, and some critics say the result is nice-looking buildings that function badly. "The works of 'starchitects' are not necessarily ill-planned or ill-detailed," writes Williams College art professor Michael J. Lewis,

> but these responsibilities are often relegated to associate firms – especially if it is an overseas commission, which comprise a large part of the practice of today's international celebrities. It is this system of collaborative partnerships, incidentally, that explains how they can handle so many commissions across the world simultaneously, each bearing the distinctive "touch" of a personal creator. It also explains the sheer overwork and overextension that can plague the busiest of the firms, with appalling consequences.[17]

Dominique Perrault's Bibliothèque Mitterrand was plagued by a variety of technical problems before and after its 1998 opening. So was Carlos Ott's Opéra Bastille, which is still under repair, 20 years after its opening. And the official report on the 2004 ceiling collapse at Paul Andreu's Terminal 2E at Charles de Gaulle Airport cited flaws in France's procedure for executing complex public projects. Andreu, then chief architect for Aéroports de Paris, was not blamed, but the report faulted a process that made it possible to avoid competition for the design and thus ensure that a showcase French project went to a French architect.

France may be proud of its architects and especially its "starchitects," but it is not especially interested in cutting-edge architecture.

XI.

Perhaps the most controversial line in my original story was this one: "Though the French music industry sold 1.7 billion dollars worth of recordings and downloads last year, few performers are famous outside the country. Quick: name a French pop star who isn't Johnny Hallyday." Armies of readers countered with examples of well-known music figures – notably composer-conductor Pierre Boulez, countertenor Philippe Jaroussky and pianist Hélène Grimaud in the field of classical music, and Manu Chao in the pop arena. A few rose to the defense of the durable Hallyday, who in his late sixties was still rocking. Such comparisons are missing the point. Though France has a few famous musicians, its place in the musical firmament has clearly declined in recent decades.

In the nineteenth and twentieth centuries, France enjoyed a commanding position in the music world. Composers like Hector Berlioz, Jacques Offenbach, Camille Saint-Saëns, Georges Bizet, Emmanuel Chabrier, Claude Debussy, Erik Satie, Maurice Ravel, and Olivier Messiaen were known the world over. Pascal Dusapin, Pierre Boulez, and Henri Dutilleux are carrying on that tradition today – though the last two, at 85 and 94 years old, respectively, have curtailed their output in recent years. In the field of popular music, Charles Trenet, Édith Piaf, Georges Brassens, Serge Gainsbourg, Juliette Gréco, and Belgian-born Jacques Brel made the *chanson française* heard 'round the world. Gréco, still performing at age 83, told me over coffee at a Paris hotel that the high point of the *chanson* was the 1950s, when artists like her and Gainsbourg were infusing the traditional form with more literate and challenging lyrics.

Then came rock 'n' roll, and France got swamped by a mostly British and American tidal wave. Hallyday struggled almost single-handedly to maintain France's honor on the world rock stage. In 1989, Culture Minister Jack Lang appointed a young music publisher named Bruno Lion as "minister of rock" to establish a French beachhead in the genre, to little avail. From the late 1950s onward, rock, the dominant music genre of the modern era, was monopolized by Britain and the U.S. France could never come up with an answer to the Beatles and the Rolling Stones, just as it still lacks a Madonna and a Radiohead – a group or artist that consistently dominates music charts almost everywhere. "France has contributed more than its fair share to Western culture," writes British music writer Claire Allfree, "but one thing it has never got its head round is rock 'n' roll."[18]

The same could be said for popular music generally. According to the polling organization Ifop, four of the 15 top-selling 2007 albums in France were by Anglo-Saxon artists (Mika, Amy Winehouse, James Blunt, and Norah Jones) and a fifth by a German band, Tokio Hotel. In the second week of February 2009, half of the 10 top albums were foreign imports (mostly from the U.S.), as well as 9 of the top 10 singles. Not one French title or artist appeared on comparable lists in the U.S. and the U.K. Nor was there a single French entry on combined lists of the best-selling albums and singles in the world. The only album by a French artist certified by the recording industry association IFPI as having sold more than 1 million copies worldwide in 2006 was Johnny Hallyday's *Ma Vérité*. Indeed, only four French singles are among the roughly 150 that have ever sold more than 5 million copies – most recently Danyel Gérard's *Butterfly*.[19] That appeared back in 1971.

To be fair, a few French pop music artists have attained success outside the Hexagon. Benin-born, Paris-based Angé-lique Kidjo, for instance, won a Grammy Award for her 2007 world music album *Djin Djin*. And France's David Guetta got a 2009 Grammy nomination for his electronic/dance album *One Love*. Indeed, France has lately dominated that particular music genre, also called techno – a blend of sampling and funk, sometimes seasoned with a bit of hip-hop (the latter usually sung in English). The French version, known as French Touch, features groups like Daft Punk, Air, Justice, and DJ-performers Guetta and Laurent Garnier, who are heard in clubs and lounges all over the world. Daft Punk's *Alive 2007* won a Grammy for best dance album and was No. 1 on the U.S. music magazine *Billboard*'s list of Top

The Death of French Culture

Electronic Albums at the end of 2007, though the recording did not sell nearly enough copies to make Billboard's list of 100 top albums from all genres.

The success of French Touch, both in France and abroad, illustrates the limits of the French government's strenuous attempts to promote homegrown popular music. Under the 1994 Toubon Law, championed by former Culture Minister Jacques Toubon, radio stations must devote 40 percent of their air time to French music, and a substantial portion of that to new groups. While the law has clearly helped some French bands get their start, it was not much of a factor in the rise of Daft Punk, Air, and most of the other top groups: what few lyrics they use are in English and thus are not helped by the law. Indeed, the prevalence of English in French pop music today would turn Toubon's remaining hair white. Every year the French music magazine *Les Inrockuptibles* asks readers to send in a demo track for its Christmas CD. Editor Jean-Daniel Beauvallet has estimated that, out of 7,000 submissions in a typical year, 6,000 are in English.[20] Why? Because English has long been the language of rock 'n' roll, and because aspiring French rock and pop musicians dream of reaching a broader audience.

That impulse led French signer Sébastien Tellier, the country's entry in the 2008 Eurovision Song Contest, to declare that he would perform in English. He was denounced by French cultural critics and politicians, at least one of whom demanded that he be replaced in the competition. (Tellier ended up singing in both English and French; he lost anyway.) Tellier's experience did not prevent the successful French chanteuse Camille from releasing an entire album in English in 2008. "Opera singers sing one day in German, one day in French, one day in English," she explained diplomatically, "and each time it's a different musical challenge. I feel the same."

Language quotas have helped one successful brand of new French music: hip-hop. It was born in the U.S. and is characterized by extensive lyrics, usually spoken or chanted rather than sung. French-language artists like Suprême NTM, IAM, and Grand Corps Malade got their start, in part, because radio stations in the 1990s were desperate for new music in French simply to meet the Toubon Law quotas. (A number of French-Canadian groups also profited.) Thus, when the Paris-based radio network Skyrock began playing hip-hop in the 1990s, ratings climbed and the station eventually shifted its entire format from rock to hip-hop.

France has done somewhat better in the field of classical music, though not so much in composition as in performance. Natalie Dessay is among the most successful sopranos in the world. Pianist Jean-Yves Thibaudet is known widely outside France for his mastery of the solo works of Erik Satie, as well as for his Vivienne Westwood-designed attire. French conductors and opera directors flourish overseas. But French composers – with the possible exceptions of U.S.-based serialist Jacques-Louis Monod and electronic-music specialist Jean Michel Jarre – generally do not. Moreover, the audience for classical music, even in France, is miniscule compared to that for other forms. Paris is one of the few world capitals without a major philharmonic concert hall. A new one is under construction at La Villette on the city's outskirts (designed by Jean Nouvel) but is not set to open until 2012.

XII.

Why has France lost its cultural leadership in the world? The reasons are complex, controversial and not as easily documented as the mere fact of decline. But just as the French have lately been questioning the performance of their country's economic model, it is appropriate that they subject their cultural viability to the same scrutiny. Decline has been a modern preoccupation in France, and its literature is rich – from Zola's *J'accuse* through Marc Bloch's wartime *Étrange défaite* (Strange Defeat) to . . . well, perhaps this book. In the past few years, we have had *Le grand gaspillage* (The Big Waste) and *La guerre des deux France* (War of the Two Frances) by historian Jacques Marseille; *L'Arrogance française* by journalists Romain Gubert and Emmanuel Saint-Martin; *Le choc de 2006* (The Shock of 2006) and *Le courage du bon sens* (The Courage of Common Sense), Michel Godet's twin critiques of the French welfare system; *Les classes moyennes à la dérive* (The Middle Class Adrift) by sociologist Louis Chauvel; Nicolas Tenzer's *Quand la France disparaît du monde* (When France Disappears from the World); and U.S. scholar Ezra Suleiman's *Schizophrénies françaises*.

Such screeds have focused mainly on economic failings, which Nicolas Sarkozy has set out to address. Cultural decline remains an elusive beast. The country has had a vague sense of unease, a kind of identity crisis, since – pick a date: 1940 and the humiliating German occupation; 1954, the start of the divisive Algerian conflict; the 1956 Suez debacle; or 1968, the revolutionary year which, conservatives like Sarkozy say, brought France under the sway of a new, dangerously self-centered generation. That cohort, complained the French weekly *Marianne* in 1998, is the source of "some of the worst evils which torment our society today." During the 2007 election campaign, Sarkozy blamed the *soixante-huitards* for – inter alia – schoolroom disorder, tolerance for criminality, bad manners, greed, excessive individualism, and rejection of the French national identity. May '68, he said, "imposed an intellectual and moral relativatism," "introduced cynicism into society and politics," and "lowered the moral level of politics." He even invoked some of the criticisms usually hurled at the right: "See how the cult of money, of short-term profit, of speculation, how the excesses of finance capitalism have been brought to us by the values of May '68." Such complaints about the decline of traditional French virtues helped inspire Sarkozy's controversial 2009 call for a grand debate on *l'identité nationale,* which he insisted would instruct the nation on the true meaning of Frenchness. Cynics, however, said it was more a ploy to prevent the far right from monopolizing fear of immigration as an electoral issue.

58

Not coincidentally, Sarkozy has described his reforms as a *politique de civilisation*. The term was borrowed from sociologist Edgar Morin, who expressed skepticism that Sarkozy knew what it meant. Philippe Manière, director of the Institut Montaigne, ventured an explanation: "Civilization is a word that has more meaning to the right, possibly because of its association with the civilizing mission of the French empire. It gives a lot of pleasure to people on the right and extreme right, and yet it cannot be criticized by the left. You can't be against civilization."[21] And in France, you cannot be taken seriously unless you support the notion that French civilization is great, synonymous with national identity – and currently in crisis. Theodore Zeldin, the Oxford University historian of France, once noted that conferences on the subject of French national identity outnumber striptease shows in Paris. Said he: "Everybody repeats that France is in crisis, in many different crises. But they seem to forget that this has always been true."[22]

One of the most sensitive aspects of France's perpetual identity crisis is the decline of its language. Though the French realize that their tongue is no longer the global medium of commerce and diplomacy, they cling to the illusion that it retains its importance as a transmitter of culture. French diplomats are forever insisting that documents at international organizations and conferences be translated into French. Jacques Chirac stormed out of a 2006 European Union meeting after his countryman Ernest-Antoine Seillière, president of the industrial confederation BusinessEurope, told the audience he would be addressing them in English. Chirac explained his walkout: "It's in the national interest, it's in the interest of culture, to maintain a cultural dialogue ... You're not going to base the world of tomorrow on a single language, a single culture."

Thus we come to one of the major reasons French culture is in decline: much of it is produced in a declining language. The combined English-speaking world is at least twice as large as its French counterpart and is growing faster. Same for the Spanish-speaking community. According to the British Council, 85 percent of international organizations use English as a working language, while only 49 percent use French.

French remains the most widely studied foreign tongue in British secondary schools, but the number of students taking it has been dropping. (It fell by 8 percent in 2006–07 alone, after the government made foreign languages noncompulsory for the GCSE certification exam.) Though French was once the most-studied foreign language in the U.S., in 2006 it accounted for only about 13 percent of university language-course enrollments, versus more than 50 percent for Spanish. Some French critics argue that Spanish should not be counted in such comparisons, since it is becoming a de facto first language in the U.S. That makes little sense. Spanish-speakers in America tend not to study their native tongue in school, having already mastered it. They want to learn English.

French retains a slippery hold in France's former colonies of Africa, the Caribbean and Asia. But there and elsewhere, the language is in retreat from an onslaught of English. Rwanda announced in 2008 that it would switch from French to English as the medium of instruction in its schools. In Vietnam, fewer than 100,000 students are taking French courses, one-tenth as many as in the 1980s. In China, French is taught at a mere 33 of the country's 15,000 secondary schools and at only 175 of its 600 largest universities. Though France promotes the spread of its language around the world, through the government-funded La Francophonie and Alliance Française, such efforts have failed to halt the slide.

What does the decline of the language mean in practical terms for French culture? Obviously, it reduces the natural audience for French literature, movies, theater and song. Translations are expensive: an average of 2,500 euros for a book of 150 pages.[23] Similar outlays are common for subtitling French movies (vastly more for dubbing with actors' voices). Besides, audiences in some countries – notably the U.S. – are famously resistant to subtitled movies. Worse still, the major organs of cultural criticism and publicity – the global buzz machine – are increasingly English-language, as well as based in the U.S. and Britain. That makes it more difficult for French artists and performers to get noticed in the wider world. "In the 1940s and '50s, everybody knew France was the center of the art scene, and you had to come here to get noticed," sociologist Alain Quemin told me. That was largely because Paris then was teeming with art dealers, critics, journals, collectors and hangers-on, all of them chattering to each other in French. Said Quemin: "Now you have to go to New York."

A second reason French culture is in decline is the French education system. Once noted for its rigor, the system is today widely criticized for its perceived emphasis on personal development at the expense of actual knowledge. In one typical critique, the 2004 book *Qui a eu cette idée folle un jour de casser l'école?* (Whose Crazy Idea Was It to Trash the School?), secondary-school teacher Fanny Capel describes, among other outrages, how educators set out to attain the official goal of 80 percent passing grades by lowering standards. One can argue about which approach to education produces the best artists, writers, and musicians, but most parents would probably opt for rigor over personal development. Indeed, it could be argued that the French system's historic rigidity once inspired much of France's now-vanished cultural vitality. "A lot of French artists were created in opposition to the education system," explains art expert Christophe Boïcos. "Romantics, Impressionists, Modernists – they were rebels against the academic standards of their day. But those standards were quite high and contributed to the impressive quality of the artists who rebelled against them."

A series of post-1968 reforms has crowded the arts out of the secondary-school curriculum. The literature baccalaureate program, once the most popular, is now far outstripped by the science and economics-sociology options. About half of all students took the Bac L in 1968, but by 2007 the figure was down to 18.6 percent. "One learns to read at school, one doesn't learn to see," complained Pierre Rosenberg, a former président-directeur of the Louvre. Or, he might have added, to think creatively. During the 2008 U.S. presidential election primaries, most major candidates called for an increase in art and music courses in the schools. One of them, former Arkansas Governor Mike Huckabee, asserted that such "right-brain" development is necessary not just to enrich the lives of students but also to inspire the creativity necessary to keep the U.S. competitive in the global economy. This from a conservative, anti-government Republican! In France, Sarkozy's Education Minister Xavier Darcos seemed to favor creativity from the other, more analytical side of the brain: "We need literate people, students who can master discourse and reasoning," he said shortly after taking office. "Those who have literary aptitudes should not have hesitations."[24]

That demand will remain unfilled without major reform of French universities, which are alarmingly overcrowded, underfinanced, disorganized, and literally falling apart. *The Times Higher Education Supplement* each year compiles a ranking of the world's 200 top universities. On the 2009 list, there were a mere four French entries: 53 from the U.S. (which accounted for 13 of the top 20), 24 from the U.K., 11 each from Canada, Japan, and the Netherlands, ten from Germany, eight from Australia, seven from Switzerland, six from China and five each from Belgium, Sweden, and Hong Kong. Only two French universities – Paris IV and the École Normale Supérieure – made it onto a 2007 *THES* list of the top 50 "arts and humanities" universities.

As educators and official reports have complained for years, France discriminates in favor of its Grandes Écoles, that handful of specialized academies that accept only the best students and virtually guarantee them a career in the upper reaches of government and business. By contrast, France's public universities, which must accept just about any local student with a baccalaureate, are starved for funds: they receive less per student than do the country's secondary schools. So much less, in fact, that hardly any French university can afford to keep its libraries open in the evening. In higher education as in so many other realms, France seems to favor the cultivation of an élite at the expense of the majority. J. R. Pitte, former president of the University of Paris IV-Sorbonne, a fine school but hardly a Grande École, wryly observed that his students enjoy an average of 2.6 sq. meters of space, while a Bresse chicken requires three times as much to retain its *Appellation d'origine contrôlée* status.

In France, education and culture are disparate worlds overseen by separate government ministries. In other countries, educational institutions are seedbeds of cultural excellence. The writing program at Britain's University of East Anglia has trained major novelists (Ian McEwan, Kazuo Ishiguro, Anne Enright), as has the one at America's University of Iowa (Wallace Stegner, James Tate, Michael Cunningham). Many leading painters and sculptors have come out of Yale University's arts program (Brice Marden, Richard Serra, Chuck Close). Germany's newly reorganized Universität der Künste Berlin is already one of the largest institutions of music and arts in the world.

And besides producing artists, universities can enrich the cultural life of a region and a nation. The 4,182 universities of the U.S. on their own house almost 700 museums, 110 publishing houses, 300 radio stations, 345 concert halls, and 2,300 performing arts centers. Harvard's American Repertory Theater has a larger budget (most of it from private sources) than many countries' national theaters. The University of Illinois's largely unsubsidized Krannert Center for the Performing Arts presents 150 dramatic works a year and has a full-time staff of nearly 90. Such institutions train not only tomorrow's artists and performers, but also the next generation of culture lovers. By starving its universities, France is missing a valuable opportunity to restore the standing of its culture.

Though it is perilous to generalize about a country of 64 million people, there is a strain in the national mindset that distrusts commercial success – as we have heard from Luc Besson. Opinion polls show that more young French aspire to government jobs than to careers in business. *Foreign Policy* magazine in 2007 published an exposé of how school

The Death of French Culture

textbooks in France (also Germany) routinely cast capitalism and entrepreneurial initiative in an unfavorable light. The story's all-too-accurate headline: "Europe's Policy of Failure." Acknowledging the problem, Education Minister Darcos in early 2008 launched a review of high school economics textbooks and curricula.

This distrust of worldly success is allied to a widespread French ambivalence about globalization. Public opinion in France has long been more hostile toward that inexorable trend than in any other European Union country. In a 2006 poll by Eurobarometer, for instance, 64 percent of French respondents called globalization "a threat." That was exactly the same percentage of Americans who, in a Harris poll a few years earlier, said the trend was good for the U.S. The contrast is especially telling, since globalization has long been identified in France as a threat made in America and aimed in particular at French culture. "The [French] governmental and intellectual élite have indeed carefully fashioned, to that end, the assertion that anything with commercial appeal (therefore potentially economically challenging) is intrinsically not 'cultural' and furthermore could erode what *is* cultural," writes Sophie M. Clavier of San Francisco State University in an unpublished 2005 paper. "There is a powerful tradition of intellectual elitism displaying nothing but contempt for commercially successful artistic endeavors, especially if such success is even in a most tenuous fashion remotely linked to American popular culture."

Curiously, France maintains an open economy for most goods and services, from the U.S. and elsewhere. Culture is another matter. In that realm, both government policy and popular perception seem to equate globalization less with economic decline than with a loss of identity. In France, culture and commerce must not mix. Says sociologist Alain Quemin: "Americans think that if artists are successful, they must be good. We think that if they're successful, they're too commercial. Success is considered bad taste." If France is to regain its cultural eminence in the world, its young artists, musicians, and writers must not be afraid of success.

XIII.

One of the most serious obstacles to France's cultural success is the government itself. As the biggest funder of and decision-maker for culture in France, the state has a virtual monopoly in that sphere, and it is not always benign. Nor is it particularly new. France has for centuries used culture as an instrument for extending influence abroad and building national cohesion at home. After World War II, a weakened nation found yet another use for this policy. "Increasingly unable to control economic trends, the French state has moved to a redefining of sovereignty from a political economic concept to a cultural one," observes Sophie M. Clavier. "If the Gaullist concepts of *prestige* and *grandeur* could not be achieved through economics, then they could be achieved through the affirmation of the strength of French culture." The result is what French sociologist Dominique Schnapper calls a "cultural welfare state," in which the government decides what culture is and which parts of it get subsidized.

France subsidizes culture more heavily, and in more ways, than just about any industrial nation. For years, French governments have aimed to devote at least 1 percent of the national budget to culture. According to the Organization for Economic Cooperation and Development (OECD), France in fact spends 1.5 percent of gross domestic product on all cultural and recreational activities, vs. only 0.7 percent for Germany, 0.5 percent for the U.K. and 0.3 percent for the U.S.

In one estimate, admittedly a few years old, France spent 29 times more per capita on culture than the U.S., a discrepancy that is no doubt higher today because of subsequent cutbacks at the U.S. National Endowment for the Arts.[25] The French Culture Ministry alone has 11,200 employees (compared to fewer than 500 for the NEA) deciding which programs, institutions, and artists receive funding. In addition, the Foreign Ministry has its own cultural budget, sending planeloads of artists, performers, and their works abroad, and subsidizing 26 research centers, 141 cultural institutes,

The Death of French Culture

176 archaeological digs, 253 French-medium high schools, and more than 1,000 French-language centers overseas. If you were a student at a U.S. university, a Foreign Ministry program would give you 1,800 dollars to put on a French film festival.

France also rigs the domestic market for culture, aiding its own practitioners and keeping out foreigners and their influences. Here are a few of the ways:

- French filmmakers can apply for an *avance sur recettes* (advance against receipts) from the Centre National de la Cinématographie, basically an interest-free loan against box office revenues. Few of the loans are ever paid back in full.
- Canal Plus, the country's leading pay-TV channel, must by law spend 20 percent of its revenues buying rights to French movies. In addition, over-the-air channels must spend 3.2 percent of their takings.
- Movies may not be issued on DVD until at least six months after their theatrical release, a policy designed to help theater owners maximize their returns.
- Proceeds from an 11 percent tax on cinema tickets are plowed back into film subsidies.
- A quota on American (and other non-European) movies limits them to 40 percent of the total number of films exhibited in France.
- French publishing houses and bookstores benefit from the *prix unique du livre*, a measure that prohibits selling new books for less than 5 percent below the listed price. In addition, the value-added tax on books is only 5.5 percent instead of the normal 19.6 percent
- By law, 40 percent of shows on TV and 40 percent of music on radio must be French. Separate quotas govern prime-time hours to ensure that French programming is not relegated to the middle of the night.
- *Intermittents du spectacle*, that is, freelance workers in the performing arts, receive special unemployment payments as if they were full-time workers.

- The vast majority of live dramatic performances in France take place in government-run or -subsidized theaters.
- Painters and sculptors can get various benefits, including subsidized studio space.

Of course, France is not alone in protecting homegrown culture. Canada and Britain have local-content requirements on some of their broadcast channels. South Korea requires cinemas to show South Korean-made films for 73 days a year. And at a Unesco meeting in 2005, France persuaded 151 countries to adopt the Convention on the Protection and Promotion of the Diversity of Cultural Expressions (only the U.S. and Israel resisted). That document enshrines the French *exception culturelle* by giving governments the right to restrict entry of foreign cultural products in their country, in the name of protecting cultural diversity.

Do all these subsidies and protections make a difference for French culture? It has surely helped some small publishers, music labels and movie studios resist the pressures of global competition. In South Korea's case, screen quotas have nurtured a film industry that is today one of the world's liveliest. By contrast, a decade after Mexico dropped its quotas in 1994 (as part of the North American Free Trade Agreement), domestic production declined from more than 100 films a year to fewer than 10.

But whether such cosseting produces great culture is debatable. Most of Mexico's pre-1994 film production consisted of low-budget "quota quickies" of dubious cinematic merit. South Korea has been reducing screen quotas in recent years as part of an effort to open its film industry to the bracing winds of competition, and the results have been positive: South Korean movies appear increasingly in Western cinemas and are perennial winners at film festivals. France's special benefits for *intermittents du spectacle* end up encouraging TV companies and other cultural institutions to avoid hiring full-time staff, which would cost considerably more in social charges. And many of those subsidized *intermittents* are technicians and clerical workers, rather than artists and performers. Protecting France's cultural industries may even have narrowed their global appeal: with quotas and a language barrier, French producers can survive without selling overseas. Why bother, when you've got a protected market at home?

Then there is the problem of *clientèlisme*, the disbursement of official favors on the basis of connections instead of merit. If French cultural policy has produced one tangible result, it is the rise of a large army of cultural bureaucrats and their counterparts at major cultural institutions. It is this inbred, élitist, Paris-centric and mostly self-perpetuating class – and not the people who actually produce and consume cultural works – who largely decide what French culture is. "One of the failings of our *exception culturelle* is that it protects our mediocre products just as well it does as our best ones," said Marc Fumaroli, a member of the French Academy who denounced such practices in his 1991 book *L'État culturel* (The Cultural State). "I speak in particular about cinema, where an excellent system – *avances sur recettes* – has too often benefitted mediocrities ... I fear that some clans have taken it over and complaisantly distributed the manna to their friends."[26]

The argument in favor of quotas and subsidies is that they maintain public goods and activities that mere market forces could not. Yet the literature of economics is rich with warnings that subsidies distort economic signals, decision-making, and resource allocation. A look at European Union agricultural policy and its perverse effects would confirm that view. In the realm of services (such as cultural activities), subsidies are criticized for promoting mediocrity and a lack of – hello! – creativity. Perhaps one of the reasons French culture fares so badly overseas is that subsidies have encouraged mediocrity and complacency among artists and performers. As British maestro Sir Thomas Beecham once said about one form of protectionism, giving employment preference to fellow citizens: "Why do we have all these third-rate foreign conductors around when we have so many second-rate ones of our own?"

The Death of French Culture

It is difficult to measure the effect of subsidies on culture. But it may be instructive to look at cultural life in a country where they are virtually nonexistent: the U.S. In his widely discussed 2006 book *De la culture en Amérique* (On Culture in America), Frédéric Martel described a U.S. cultural scene of surprising depth and vigor. A former cultural attaché at the French Embassy in Boston, Martel spent five years interviewing more than 700 American cultural figures and visiting theaters, museums, and opera companies across the country. Instead of a cultural wasteland of I-Pods and *Desperate Housewives*, he found an America that has roughly as many artists and theaters per capita as France, and even more libraries, dance companies, and cinemas. Americans, he discovered, are on average just as likely as the French to have read a book, visited a museum, seen a film, or gone to a concert in the past year. (Others have noted that as many Americans attend live opera performances as National Football League games.) And all this without significant government funding or bureaucracy. Writes Martel: "If the Ministry of Culture is nowhere, culture is everywhere."

The difference, he found, is that American cultural institutions rely heavily on individual and corporate donations, private-foundation support, tax deductions, and innovative fund-raising techniques, rather than government subsidies. It helps that the U.S. economy in recent decades has had higher growth rates than those of France. Accordingly, the displacement of Paris as a center of the art world has much to do with the pre-eminence of New York City and London as major financial centers, with their legions of wealthy, arts-minded donors and buyers. (And for that reason, Beijing and Shanghai, Dubai and Doha are on the rise as cultural capitals.) State and local governments in the U.S. also support the arts, directly and indirectly, but most decisions are made locally by cultural institutions and their supporters. "There is no pilot in the plane," Martel writes of the U.S. system. "There is neither a central authority nor a supreme decision-maker. No regulations to speak of. Instead, there is something better: thousands of independent actors, working in

69

concert with each other." The result is a culture that is just as strong as France's, even in its more élite forms like opera and classical music, but more diverse and more responsive to the interests of its audience. Concludes Martel: "Such is the miracle of civic cultural humanism." France could use a miracle like that.

XIV.

Can French culture be saved? Not without some hard work. One place to begin is the educational system. Encouragingly, the Sarkozy government has proposed more art-history teaching in secondary schools. But why not additional music, literature, and practical art courses too? More students should be encouraged to pursue the literature baccalaureate, perhaps by selling them on the career-enhancing benefits of mastering communications and reasoning skills.

More English-language instruction would help as well. Like it or not, France must face the cold fact that the language of international cultural discourse today is English. If French artists, writers, and musicians are unable to master it, their horizons will remain confined to a small Gallic village. In fact, internationally successful French artists – from conductor Pierre Boulez to artist Pierre Huyghe – do use English on an almost daily basis and realize that it is essential for communicating with their international constituencies. (My wife interviewed Huyghe for an article in *Time* and attests that his English is excellent.) Filmmakers like Luc Besson and Mathieu Kassovitz have hit on a promising strategy: make the movies in English, then dub them into French for the domestic market. French pop stars have taken that one step further: sing in English, and forget about a French version. Language purists will have heart attacks, but if France wants to be a major cultural exporter, its works have to be export-ready.

Some commentators have proposed that the Culture and Education ministries be merged. That move may not solve many problems by itself, but it would certainly send a message to young people that knowing and appreciating culture is an integral part of being educated. And here is a radical thought: Why not take some of those under-employed, subsidized artists and *intermittents du spectacle* and put them into the schools as part-time teachers, advisers, and artists-in-residence? (By some estimates, 18 percent of Parisians receiving unemployment compensation are artists.) That would expose more students not just to culture, but to the people who actually make it – and perhaps those role models could help turn the French education system once again into an incubator of artistic talent.

France's universities could use a similar makeover. More money would help, of course, as would more control for individual campuses over their finances, curricula, and admissions policies. The imbalance between the universities and the Grandes Écoles is now so widely decried that reform may at last be possible. Though perhaps not imminent: A recent government proposal to admit more students from modest backgrounds to the Grandes Écoles has met stiff resistance from the schools' directors and alumni. Only one such institution, Sciences Po, the former École Libre des Sciences Politiques, has made a serious effort to democratize its student population. Encouragingly, the Sarkozy government has made private donations to educational institutions partly tax deductible. (That's fine, but why not fully deductible?) The government in 2009 also gave 20 of its largest universities a measure of autonomy over spending. But more reform is needed, including increased emphasis in the curriculum on such "right-brain" subjects as art, literature, and music. If other countries can use higher education to promote both innovation and cultural excellence, surely France can.

Just about any reform of France's cultural infrastructure will require more money. New sources of income will have to be found for the country's cultural institutions if they are to survive. The experience of the U.S., Britain, and other countries has shown that there are alternatives to direct government grants – such as public-private partnerships and donations from individuals. Governments from Britain to Tennessee have come up with innovative ways outside the tax system to fund cultural activities, from lotteries to hotel-room surcharges to special fees for automobile license plates.

Is it too much to ask of France that it develop the habits of philanthropy that exist elsewhere? On a per capita basis, the British give five times more to charity than the French do, the Americans ten times more. Even wealthy French who sit on the country's various cultural boards rarely contribute money to their own institutions. There is room for improvement, especially if the government adopts the kind of tax incentives that other countries have used to encourage donations. One suggestion is to make private contributions to cultural and other charitable organizations fully and immediately deductible from a donor's taxable income. "In the U.S. you can donate a painting to a museum and take a full deduction," says art expert Christophe Boïcos. "Here it's limited. Here the government makes the important decisions. But if the private sector got more involved and cultural institutions got more autonomy, France could undergo a major artistic revival."

Sarkozy's appointment of Christine Albanel as his first Culture Minister was seen as a vote in favor of individual initiative: as director of Versailles, she cultivated private donations and partnerships with businesses, and she pledged to extend such practices. Her successor, Frédéric Mitterrand, a nephew of the former President, is a cultural veteran of more conventional, statist views. Nonetheless, private participation is advancing. The Festival d'Avignon now relies on private and corporate contributions for about 5 percent of its budget, a figure its organizers hope to increase. The Louvre has announced it will establish an endowment to supplement the museum's government funding. In an unusual display of entrepreneurship, the Louvre also plans to open offshoots in Atlanta and Abu Dhabi. The French are often suspicious of greater corporate involvement in culture, though it has worked well in other countries without adverse effects on institutional independence. And even in the U.S., where corporate underwriting is perhaps most robust, it amounts to only 2.5 percent of all arts spending, hardly enough to arouse alarm.

The French are not likely to show much financial generosity toward their cultural institutions as long as the government's deep pockets are always available. Sarkozy in 2009 formed a council of cultural eminences to consider "recentering the support for excellence," a euphemism for reducing government subsidies. He also announced a new government initiative to promote French culture abroad, replacing Culturesfrance with a network of cultural centers branded the Agence Victor Hugo, similar to Spain's Instituto Cervantes, Germany's Goethe-Institut, China's Confucius Institute and the British Council. As of early 2010, however, he was having trouble finding someone to spearhead the effort. The leading candidate, author Charles Ruffin, Ambassador to Senegal and a member of the French Academy, declined the job, reportedly because its goals and resources were too vague, and some French ambassadors objected to giving up control over their embassies' culture budgets.

French cultural policy has long been geared more toward encouraging the production of cultural products at home rather than their distribution overseas. Oddly, the government acknowledged in early 2009 that it had reduced its funding for Foreign Ministry culture programs abroad by 20 percent, with even deeper cuts to such seemingly productive efforts as book translation and film distribution. (Britain, Germany, Spain and China, meanwhile, have been expanding their cultural outreach activities.) A wiser strategy would be to focus on raising French culture's profile abroad while reducing the government's role in determining what gets produced in France.

In any case, changing old habits of dependency will require a major withdrawal of government from the cultural space, a politically difficult undertaking. Margaret Thatcher was able to reduce government funding of the arts in Britain, but Tony Blair – recognizing the political gains to be had –

restored some of the cuts and even funded free admissions to major museums. In France, a 2000 Ifop poll for *L'Express* magazine found that 57 percent of French people approved of a strong government role in protecting and subsidizing culture. President Sarkozy in early 2009 affirmed his belief in a powerful Culture Ministry, prompting its former head, Jean-Jacques Aillagon, to observe wryly: "The alliance of state and culture makes one think of the mystical marriage between Venice and the sea celebrated each year by the Doge." Nonetheless, by making culture virtually a government monopoly, France risks fostering a myopic view of that sea as the near-exclusive preserve of bureaucrats and Parisian élites.

There are some things France cannot do by itself: other countries need to change their thinking. The U.S., Britain, and Germany in particular are so focused on their own enormous cultural output that they unjustly ignore France's. Though Germany's Kunst Kompass is widely accepted as a measure of artistic standing in the world, foreign critics say it gives exceptional weight to German artists' expositions, publications, and museums. In addition, the myopia of the English language and its native speakers is a scandal. "It is particularly painful," says Esther Allen of Columbia University, "to observe that when it comes to literature, [English] does indeed behave more like an invasive species than a lingua franca, resisting and supplanting whatever is not written in itself, speaking in the loudest of voices while failing to pay much attention at all to anything said in another language." Indeed, the term "British art" appeared 111 times in Britain's *Guardian* newspaper in 2009 versus the 13 times that "French art" was mentioned. Says Guy Walter, director of the Villa Gillet cultural center in Lyon: "When I point out a great new French novel to a New York publisher, I am told it's 'too Frenchy.' But Americans don't read French, so they don't really know." France can help them know by expanding its cultural and language promotion effort overseas. That is one cultural function of government that does not stifle creativity at home.

The Death of French Culture

What those foreigners are missing is that French culture is surprisingly lively. France's movies, for instance, are becoming more imaginative and accessible. Consider such intelligent yet popular works as Rachid Bouchareb's *Indigènes* (Days of Glory) and Jacques Audiard's *Un Prophèt,* both hits on the foreign art-house circuit and both nominated for Oscars. Or look at Tunisian-born Abdellatif Kechiche's well-crafted films: his last two, *L'Esquive* (Games of Love and Chance) and *La Graine et le mulet* (Couscous), each won the César, France's national film award, for best picture.

Meanwhile, French novelists are focusing increasingly on the here and now: one of the big books of the 2007 season, Olivier Adam's *A l'abri de rien* (In the Shadow of Nothing) concerns immigrants at the Sangatte refugee camp. Even Culturesfrance's Olivier Poivre d'Arvor produced a 2008 novel, *Le voyage du fils,* based on the immigrant experience. Éric Zemmour, Philippe Besson, and Mazarine Pingeot have turned recent news stories into novels, inspiring controversy and even lawsuits. Maxime Chattam's *Prédateurs* proved that French writers can compete with the Anglo-Saxons in the thriller genre. Patrick Chamoiseau, Tahar Ben Jelloun, Yasmina Khadra, Anna Moï, and Alain Mabanckou have enriched French letters with linguistic zest from France's overseas territories, its former colonies, and other exotic climes. Indeed, the Prix Goncourt, perhaps France's top literary award, was given in 2008 to Afghan-born Atiq Rahimi and in 2009 to Marie N'Diaye, born in France of a French mother and Senagalese father. Another top prize, the Renaudot, went in 2008 to Tierno Monénembo, a "francophone" writer from Guinea. With time, such sons and daughters of the old empire might even take the same commanding role on the world literary stage currently held by writers from the former British colonies, such as India's Rohinton Mistry, Vikram Seth, Vikram Chandra, Romesh Gunesekera, Arundhati Roy, Pankaj Mishra, Anita and Kiran Desai, Bangladesh's Taslima Nasreen, Pakistan's Bapsi Sidwa, Britain's (Indian-born) Salman Rushdie and Hanif Kureishi, and America's (British-born) Jhumpa Lahiri and Pico Iyer.

The Death of French Culture

France's Japan-influenced graphic novels have made their country a leader in the "ninth art," one of literature's hottest genres. Indeed, more than 4,700 French *bandes dessinées* were published in 2008, up 10 percent from the year before.[27] Total sales hit 320 million euros, thanks partly to new entries in the popular *Titeuf, Blake et Mortimer,* and *Lucky Luke* series. That output makes France a bigger producer of original graphic novels than the U.S.

In music, meanwhile, singers like Benjamin Biolay, Bénabar, Vincent Delerm, Camille, and Zazie have helped revive the *chanson*. Artists like Abd al Malik, a son of Congolese immigrants, Senegal-born MC Solaar, Cyprus native Diam's and the Guadeloupean transplant known as Doc Gynéco have taken the lingo of the streets and turned it into a sharper, more poetic version of American rap. Though French rap commands little respect from the country's élites, it represents one of France's most vibrant cultural genres. It opens a rare avenue of artistic expression to denizens of the crumbling, racially segregated *banlieues*.

And there may reside the hope for France's return to global glory. The country's angry, ambitious minorities are ready to commit culture all over the place. Despite its quotas and subsidies, France is becoming a multiethnic bazaar of art, music, and writing from the *banlieues*, as well as from disparate corners of the nonwhite world beyond. African, Asian, and Latin American music get more retail space in France than perhaps any other country. Movies from Afghanistan, Argentina, Hungary and other distant lands fill the cinemas. "On any day, about five times as many foreign films, past or present, are screened in Paris as in any other city on earth," wrote British academic Perry Anderson in a lengthy 2004 appraisal of French standing in the world. "Much of what is now termed 'world cinema' – Iranian, Taiwanese, Senegalese – owes its visibility to French consecration and funding. Had directors like [Abbas] Kiarostami, Hou Xiao Xien or [Ousmane] Sembene depended on reception in the Anglo-American world, few outside their native lands would ever have glimpsed them."[28]

Likewise, courageous publishers, such as Actes Sud's Hubert Nyssen and the late Christian Bourgeois, allow authors of all nations to be translated into French and, inevitably, they will influence the next generation of French writers. That has long been the case: Proust immersed himself in the works of Britain's John Ruskin before writing his *À la recherche du temps perdu*. Dostoyevsky decided to become a novelist after reading Balzac's *Eugénie Grandet*. And not all of those French writers of the future will have been born there. "France has always been a country where people could come from any country and immediately start painting or writing in French – or even not in French," says Marjane Satrapi, an Iranian whose movie based on her graphic novel *Persepolis* was France's 2008 Oscar entry in the Best Foreign Film category. "The richness of French culture is based on that quality."

In other countries, notably the U.S. and the U.K., racial and ethnic minorities participate more fully in cultural life, and cultural institutions strive hard for diversity in their programs, their audience, and the artists they use. In France, such *métissage* was popular in smart circles a decade or so ago. Today, it is dismissed as an old fad, and cultural mandarins seem to favor a single version of French culture that pretty much excludes immigrant influences. Sarkozy's harping on the purity of *l'identité nationale* has not helped. The Comédie Française had to cancel its 2007 production of Bernard-Marie Koltès's *Retour au désert* (Back to the Desert) after the playwright insisted that the role of the servant Aziz be played by an Arab. Embarrassingly, there was not a single actor of Arab origin in the company's 56-member troupe, though an estimated 8 percent of France's population has Arab roots.

Perhaps it was no accident that Olivier Poivre d'Arvor's list of 300 prominent French cultural figures did not include Saïd Taghmaoui, one of the most successful French actors in Hollywood *(The Kite Runner*, TV's *West Wing)*. The son of Moroccan immigrants, Taghmaoui told *Newsweek* he left France because, "As a minority actor in France, you often

The Death of French Culture

wind up playing the buffoon."[29] Author Frédéric Martel, for one, has denounced what he calls the "hypocrisy" of France's support for the *exception culturelle*. As he explained it to me: "Americans defend cultural diversity at home and deny it around the world. France defends cultural diversity around the world but denies it at home."

And what keeps a nation great if not the infusion of new energy from the margins? "America isn't dominant just because it has an imperialistic culture," says Martel, "but because it has become, with all its minorities, the world in miniature." Consider the recent rise of Berlin as a cultural capital. That probably has less to do with its (exceedingly modest) role as a global financial capital than with its abundance of cheap real estate, a consequence of the fall of the Berlin Wall and the sudden availability of vast acres of decrepit, underpopulated residential neighborhoods in eastern Berlin. Into them have flowed a tidal wave of immigrants, from abroad and from within Germany – many of them artists. Just as Paris thrived as an artistic center in the last century because of its raffish, affordable Montmartres and Montparnasses, the new cultural vanguard emerges from society's margins and fills its vacuums. Thus did the young Spaniard Pablo Picasso find Paris a welcoming place, as did Russian refugees Serge Diaghilev, Vassily Kandinsky and Marc Chagall, and all those émigré photographers featured in the 2009 Hôtel de Sully show.

Expand the definition of culture a bit, and you'll find two fields in which France excels by absorbing outside influences. First, France is arguably the world leader in fashion, thanks to the sharp antennae of its cosmopolitan designers, from Coco Chanel and Pierre Cardin to Anne Valérie Hash, Jean-Paul Gautier, and Christian Lacroix. French fashion houses truly know no borders. British designers John Galliano, Stella McCartney, and the late Alexander McQueen have created collections for Christian Dior, Chloé and Givenchy, respectively, while Israel's Alber Elbaz has worked for Lanvin, American Marc Jacobs has designed for Louis Vuitton, and

German-born Karl Lagerfeld has conjured visions for Chanel. In some ways, fashion today is what the larger cultural landscape is becoming: a truly international marketplace where nationality means little, creativity everything. One of the reasons for France's fashion success on this playing field is the almost total absence of subsidies and cultural bureaucrats.

Second, French cuisine – built on Italian foundations (a fact denied by many French) and enriched by other foreign infusions – remains the global standard, though competition is increasing from such quarters as Britain, Japan, and the U.S. Nicolas Sarkozy in 2008 proposed that French cuisine be protected under UNESCO's World Heritage rubric. That is a misguided notion. French cuisine is not a museum piece to be preserved in aspic, but a living, fast-evolving organism whose strength is its mutability. In a related field, wine, French producers are adopting techniques developed abroad – cold fermentation, micro-oxygenation, and, above all, aggressive marketing – to retain their reputation for excellence in the face of competition from wine-growing regions of the New World. France was overtaken by Italy in 2008 as the world's biggest wine producer in terms of volume, but that had much to do with French producers' new focus on restricting yield to improve quality. Tellingly, many French vines were long ago grafted onto disease-resistant rootstocks from, of all places, the U.S. The parallels with culture are obvious. "We have to take the risk of globalization," says Villa Gillet's Guy Walter. "We must welcome the outside world."

The outside world has raised its game. Unlike a century ago, France is now competing for attention on the global cultural stage with filmmakers from Iran and South Korea, musicians from Japan and Eastern Europe, writers from India and Mexico (and, in recent years, Nobel literature prize winners from Turkey and South Africa). The rising nations of Asia, in particular, are coming on strong. Consider the Chinese literary scene, almost moribund two decades ago but now thriving. *Wolf Totem*, a 2004 novel by a Beijing professor named Jiang Rong, sold 20 million copies in China and is being published in 24 other countries. Chinese film stars (Jackie Chan, Gong Li, Zhang Ziyi) and pop musicians (Faye Wong, Jay Chow, Sun Yue) are household names all over Asia. Pop culture has become a vehicle for China to exercise its "soft power" throughout Asia and, soon, the West. China severely restricts imports of foreign cultural products, mostly for ideological reasons. But those restrictions have been loosening in recent years, and foreign films now account for as much as two-thirds of Chinese box office receipts. China's contemporary art scene is one of the world's most robust, with works by homegrown artists going for millions of dollars at auction. And splendid new buildings have been rising in Beijing and Shanghai with architectural daring that would frighten most French politicians. Chinese culture is filtering through Asia as an indirect result of the country's preference for economic and cultural relations over military might. Chinese CDs and DVDs, legal and otherwise, are sold on street corners all over the developing world, even where Chinese is not widely spoken.

Asia is also a powerhouse in Western classical music, and its performers now dominate music academies and concert halls throughout the West. "The rise of the middle class in Japan after World War II, South Korea after the Korean War, and China after the Cultural Revolution made it possible for many Asians to pursue music at an advanced level," says Mari Yoshihara, the Japanese-American author of a 2007 book on the subject, *Musicians from a Different Shore*. "The successful implementation of musical pedagogy such as Suzuki Method in the second half of the twentieth century also played an important role in making classical music a widespread middle-class pursuit." As the Asian middle class grows increasingly prosperous and numerous, it will become both a producer and a consumer of culture. Likewise, Venezuela's El Sistema, a highly successful, 35-year-old program for identifying and training classical-music talent, has been copied by two dozen countries. France, among other

Western nations, will be facing serious competition. The bar is being raised.

France excels on one important global yardstick: quality of life. The country ranks among the top 10 on the United Nations' Human Development Index, even though per capita income is barely in the top 20. France's lively cultural scene is clearly one of its assets. A number of foreign-born cultural figures – American conductor William Christie, German sculptor Anselm Kiefer, novelists Dai Sijie of China and Andreï Makine of Russia – have chosen to live and work here (as have I). If France can maintain its vaunted government services during the current economic crisis – better yet, if it softens its income tax rates and abolishes a self-defeating excise on a resident's worldwide wealth – there is no reason the country cannot attract more cultural figures, and even lure back some it has lost. Like it or not, France is in a worldwide competition for artistic talent. Says Sandrine Voillet, presenter of the 2007 BBC television series *Sandrine's Paris*: "Location is becoming irrelevant to cultural production. Artists are creating all over the world, meeting other artists all over the world, and sending their art all over the world."

In 1946, Jean-Paul Sartre wrote to thank the U.S. for Ernest Hemingway, William Faulkner, and other writers who were then influencing French fiction – but whom Americans were starting to neglect. "We shall give back to you these techniques which you have lent us," he promised. "We shall return them digested, intellectualized, less effective, and less brutal – consciously adapted to French taste. Because of this incessant exchange, which makes nations rediscover in other nations what they have invented first and then rejected, perhaps you will rediscover in these new [French] books the eternal youth of that 'old' Faulkner."[30]

Thus will the world discover the eternal youth of France, a nation whose long quest for glory has honed a fine appreciation for the art of borrowing. When the more conventional

The Death of French Culture

minds of the French cultural Establishment stop imposing their own vision of culture on the nation and start applauding the ferment on the fringes, France will reclaim its reputation as a cultural power. And then some American newsmagazine will publish a cover story on "The Rebirth of French Culture."

2

The Trappings of Greatness

Antoine Compagnon

When Jules Grévy opened the annual Salon of painting around 1880, he asked whether it was a success. "Nothing all that wonderful," he was told, "but a good average." The President rubbed his hands. "A good average! Excellent! That's what we need in a democracy." Grévy, a blasé opportunist, would soon be resigning when it was discovered that his son-in-law was selling the Legion of Honor, but he was in advance of his time. We have long thought ourselves to be the best, but France these days is an average cultural power – a good average cultural power.

Still, we fell to earth with quite a bump when, in December 2007, in headlines on the front cover of the European edition of *Time*, we learned of "the death of French culture." Even worse, the American edition that came out that same week carried a different cover, and Donald Morrison's article wasn't even included.

The fact is that this news – nothing less than the Fall of the House of France – isn't of the kind that the sales executives of *Time* deem likely to interest their national readers. Seen from the United States, or at least as the expectations of its audience are imagined by Time Warner (that big cultural battalion that also includes AOL, HBO, and CNN), the demise of French culture is an open-and-shut case – and that means the obliteration of France *tout court*, since, up to the present day, no country has identified itself to such an extent with its culture. And the corpse has had all the time it needs to grow cold. Only Europeans may still be bothered by this information (which the Asian edition of *Time*, following the controversy, did actually pick up on the following month). And this means the French first and foremost, but also their European partners, who clearly need to be advised of the way their pretentious neighbor has run aground.

Actually, beyond the trenchant title and the flashy cover, Donald Morrison's article contained no new information and divulged no scandalous revelation. Who would deny that French culture – literature, film, painting, and even fashion design, cuisine, and wine – is no longer exported as easily as in the past? Or that it no longer enjoys the standing that traditionally put anything made in Paris in a class of its own? Or that other cultures – not just European, but also American, Asian, and African cultures – are stealing some of its market share? This was really nothing to write home about.

Nonetheless, shortly after the publication of that fateful issue of *Time*, *Le Monde* asked me to give my reactions. Why not? I was just passing through Paris, during a prolonged stay in New York. It was an opportunity to give my view – realistic if not pessimistic – on our culture's strike power. Far from rejecting Donald Morrison's disappointed diagnostic wholesale, I smoothed out some of its edges, I pointed out a few exceptions. And I showed little enthusiasm for the multicultural remedies that he prescribed for us if we were to get back on our feet. My opinion was the first to appear in the columns of the French press.[1] Then I left for New York, without any inkling of the hullabaloo that the cover of the American magazine was about to unleash in France – or rather in one or two arrondissements on the Left Bank – for several weeks toward the end of 2007, until the usual Christmas-New Year holiday lull.

From New York, I observed the avalanche of reactions. Overall, there was a sense of scandalized indignation as people vehemently protested against the cruel way in which

Donald Morrison had nailed French culture. They had done the same three years before, when the *London Review of Books* published two scathing articles by the Marxist sociologist Perry Anderson on "The Fall of France."[2] I rapidly realized that I had been pretty much the only person not to disagree entirely with the *Time* journalist, even though I wasn't completely convinced by his argument. The international influence of French culture may indeed be diminishing, but this is probably because, for the time being, it has lost its ability to come out of itself and take a look at the world around it. But if French culture is in crisis, it is not for the first time, and other cultures – notably that of America – are in the same position. And a crisis can be a good thing if you emerge from it stronger. There were more and more radio and television broadcasts on the subject; I was invited to some of them. Luckily I wasn't able to accept the invitations: I would have found myself caught between the hammer and the anvil.

I returned to Paris after the battle, and here I found quite a few letters waiting in my in-tray – many more than when I express an opinion in the newspapers on universities, research, or the school system – attacking my think-piece in *Le Monde*. Mostly, the writers of these letters were driven by an overt anti-Americanism that is endemic in France.[3] One of my sentences had particularly annoyed them: the one in which – acknowledging, with Donald Morrison, that the contemporary French novel had only a modest appeal – I admitted that I was happier reading "the latest Philip Roth, Pynchon or DeLillo than the latest self-reflexive fiction concocted in Saint-Germain-des-Prés, the latest minimalist drollery or post-naturalist school exercise." This had got up the noses of my correspondents, but it was the allusion to Philip Roth that really made them see red (I suppose the two other names didn't mean anything to them), and they brandished the name of this or that rarefied, genteel, inoffensive French writer at me, all in the name of the defense of the French language: "I'd swap all the turgid, stodgy works of Roth – none of which I've ever managed to finish – for a few of Paul

Trappings of Greatness

Maçon's charming pages on a sunset at Châteauroux," one of them wrote me.

This brought home to me how out-of-kilter my position had been with respect to the near-unanimity of French opinion. Keeping my distance from the original attack as much as from the ripostes coming from the cultural intermediaries of Paris, I found that I had fallen between two stools, into the place occupied by the double agent, the turncoat, or even the traitor: I was a Frenchman who had gone over to the enemy; I had kept my political opinions to myself; I refused to march to the front with a flower in the barrel of my rifle. This was what some of my most brazen correspondents said of me.

Why had I instinctively felt so out of step with the imminent French counter-offensive? In fact, if I'd waited for a few days before reacting, if I hadn't reacted until I discovered how touchy French opinion was, or until I'd observed how very defensive we become when faced with any attack from outside, I wouldn't have been able to utter an opinion at all, since I'd have been forced deliberately to dissociate myself from my compatriots, to weigh up the pros and cons, to produce a subtler, more dialectical response. Let's accept that the best of what France produces on the international scene should be defended: this is still no reason to remain blind to her weaknesses.

It is this solitary ordeal that now forces me to re-examine, first of all, my own situation with regard to French culture, to American culture, and to the risk that they may both collapse. I need to reflect on my longstanding ambivalence about the relations between France and America – an ambivalence that I generally keep well repressed, but that on this occasion has blown up in my face. Once I've settled that particular score, I'll pursue my discussion with Donald Morrison – not by brandishing any Defense and Illustration of French Culture at him,[i] but by attempting to take up a position outside the caricatures prevalent on both sides. For I must admit that I feel no solidarity either with the American indictment of French culture as expressed in *Time*, or with the French speech for the defense, whether it is formulated by the ancients or by the moderns, by the defenders of "culture for everyone," such as Maurice Druon of the French Academy, former Minister for Cultural Affairs, or by the defenders of "culture *by* everyone," such as Olivier Poivre d'Arvor, the director of Culturesfrance.[ii] There are both objective and subjective reasons for my solitude in the face of a holy alliance of French opinion from *Le Figaro* to *Libération*, mustered in the defense of national culture. Let's start with the subjective reasons.

1.

If I rarely intervene on subjects that involve Franco-American relations, this is because I happen to know that the two cultures almost inevitably misunderstand each other.

Only once did I publish an article on the condition of French literary studies in the United States, nearly twenty years ago,[4] and I've regretted it ever since. In it, I described the increasingly ideological and limited character of those studies – the result of the watchwords of cultural diversity, identity politics, and pride in one's community. It was an article that went against the trend, and it was long held against me. This time, I sensed the same misunderstanding, but the other way round. The problem, when you have lived for too long between two cultures – as is my case with France and the United States – is that you no longer entirely belong to either, so that distance and irony become inevitable. As the years went by, I saw so many French people write knowingly about America after a brief sojourn in New York or a lightning visit to California, and so many Americans in Paris cashing in on their gourmet tours around Montparnasse or the Marais, that I preferred to stay aloof.

I bear a very French name that clearly alludes to its roots among the common people, to an old working-class tradition: it is a name that, as for so many other French men and women, designates the rise in social class that has in modern times been possible thanks to education. For nearly 35 years I have taught French literature, in France and outside it, in "sites of memory" at the heart of the nation such as the Sorbonne or the Collège de France. And yet I do not feel French – not properly. To begin with, I wasn't born in France; my mother wasn't French; the greater part of my childhood and teens was spent far away from the "mother country." Don't misunderstand me: I am not, in saying this, laying claim to any difference, any multicultural status – both of which, these days, are signs of distinction when you come from the South or the East. This is far from being my case, since no other country apart from France has left its mark on me as much as the United States. I arrived there for the first time in 1962, on board the liner *France* – what a name! the symbol of a country that still took itself to be a great power – on the eve of the Cuban missile crisis, which was my initiation into America. Ever since then, I have been forever coming and going between the two sides of the Atlantic.

I was in America on September 22, 1963, the day John F. Kennedy was assassinated. We were just coming out of lunch when we learned the news from a friend at my high school in Washington, D.C., who had just heard it on his car radio (the students parked their cars in the school parking lot). We started discussing it heatedly on the lawn, then we were sent home, downhearted. In the bus we pondered how power would be handed over, with Vice-President Lyndon Johnson succeeding the murdered president.

I was in America on September 11, 2001. I'd returned a few days earlier: New York had never looked so beautiful as seen from the plane window before we touched down at JFK on a cloudless sunny day. A friend from downtown called me at 9 o'clock on the dot, having just seen with his own eyes the first plane crashing into the North Tower. I switched on the television to watch CNN, and saw the second plane plunge into the other tower, with all that ensued – the men and women flinging themselves out of the windows, the collapse of the towers, the list of the missing. That evening, New

York was a dead city. I walked up Madison Avenue, right in the middle of the street: there wasn't a single vehicle on it, and I was like a man alone in a city blasted by an atom bomb.

When you've lived in the United States, experiencing the assassination of Kennedy and 9/11, and when you've been a teenager there and your school friends have gone off to Vietnam, you're not altogether the same person. I haven't experienced any equivalent dates in the history of France. I remember May 13, 1958, one of my first political memories: I can still hear De Gaulle's speech, with my mother glued to the radio as she listened.[iii] In May 1968, I was confined to a provincial boarding school. On May 10, 1981 – it's always May – I was again out of France.[iv]

In the United States, I've also experienced several absurd moments of anti-French hysteria: in 1965, when De Gaulle announced the French withdrawal from NATO; in 1986, when France refused to open its skies to American bombers on their way to Libya; and, of course, in 2003, when Jacques Chirac threatened to use France's veto against the Iraq war at the U.N. Security Council. Those were difficult moments to live through, but there were much happier times for France and culture, as when Malraux took the *Mona Lisa* across to Jacqueline Kennedy and the Americans. At that time, art and high culture still coexisted happily with luxury and the fashion industry, without offending democratic sensibilities. Disguised as a bellboy from Maxim's with a little red hat, I passed round a cigarette tray at the embassy receptions when the Théâtre de France – "France" yet again – made its annual rounds. The word "France" still carried weight in the New World, with the liner, or the Odéon theater that Malraux had presented to Jean-Louis Barrault under the name Théâtre de France. Genet's *The Screens*, then May '68, would soon disturb this luxury, this calm: we were dancing on a volcano.

In short, here, I am definitively catalogued as pro-American. A large part of my family and of my life link me to the United States. And yet, I don't fit in there any more than I do in France. In any case, I don't claim to know the U.S. apart from the East Coast. I've been across it twice by car, the first time through the north, the second time through the center. I've been to over half of the states, but I've only passed through, and basically I feel at home only in New York, a city that is barely American, and is hated by most Americans – a global metropolis that gathers all the diasporas into itself, an extremity of Europe and a headland of the south jutting into the north. On several occasions, I've turned down jobs in other places, in the south, west, and east of the U.S., on fine, spruce campuses.

And I do not idealize America. What I love about it is the Constitution, the First Amendment, democracy, freedom, the respect for the rule of law. What I hate about it is the intolerance and censorship that are always ready to raise their heads again, from *The Scarlet Letter* to McCarthyism, and even the "culture wars" under the first President Bush, the attacks on civil liberties in the wake of September 11, and the "Patriot Act" of October 2001.

In the course of a seasonal Franco-American migration that has lasted for a long time now, the worst year was indisputably 2002–03, with the harsh autumn (especially in New York) of preparations for war and elections to the Congress, then the terrible spring (especially in Paris) of the Iraq invasion and anti-American demonstrations under cover of protests against the war. I was filled with intense unease; on both sides of the Atlantic, I wished I could disappear. Autumn was horrible, because American opinion and the American press had not yet reacted against the self-censorship that the "war on terror" had imposed on them: not just enlightened dailies such as the *New York Times*, but also the "liberal" (in the American sense) reviews such as *The New Republic*, had become unreadable. The Democrats, afraid that the slightest criticism of the diplomatic and strategic efforts of George W. Bush might lay them open to the accusation of being unpatriotic and lead to their losing the November elections, played the ostrich rather than the donkey. A public discourse focused entirely on "weapons of mass destruction" – the presence of which we have since learned was false – was draped over everything like a leaden cloak, and even on university campuses there was no alternative.

Then, on my return to France, I failed to espouse the sole mentality prevalent at that time, and I must have been one of the few French people not to applaud to the rafters when Dominique de Villepin gave his speech to the Security Council of the United Nations in February 2003. Not that I supported the war, or that I was in favor of the democratic reshaping of the "Greater Middle East"; rather, the threat of a French veto was diplomatically counterproductive. On the day the Americans invaded Iraq, March 20, 2003, I was just about to start my class at the Sorbonne when a student asked me if he could make an announcement. I agreed. He called on his fellow students to demonstrate against the war outside the United States Embassy, on the Place de la Concorde. When he had finished, I told them to make sure they weren't demonstrating in favor of a tyrant: but the slogans uttered on that day and the gatherings that followed – gatherings that were not only anti-American, but sometimes also anti-Semitic – would only increase my sense of malaise in this, the worst of my Franco-American experiences.

Since then, the American press has rallied, with the revelation of the scandal of Abu Ghraib by the *New Yorker* in April 2004, and then the investigations carried out by the *New York Times* into the fiction of weapons of mass destruction that had been the pretext for the invasion of Iraq. The political class also got a grip on itself, as did America as a whole, even if the country did not abandon the war in Iraq, with the result that its image in the world was tarnished for the foreseeable future. But with the election of Barack Obama in 2008 – the French edition of this book was published in the course of his presidential campaign – American society and its political system once again proved their extraordinary capacity for self-regulation. It is impossible to ignore this context if we are to understand the way that an American attack on French culture was received in France.

2.

The second, and perhaps more objective, reason for my not foreseeing the vehemence of French reactions to Donald Morrison's article was that his diagnosis seemed to me, generally speaking, correct, at least when it came to literature, cinema, or the plastic arts, and even though he could be criticized for various omissions (especially the way he ignores the well-deserved successes of several French musicians and architects abroad). In any case, Donald Morrison was simply repeating facts often repeated in France itself, including in a large number of official documents. Admittedly, I hadn't paid any attention to the magazine cover, featuring a sort of teary-eyed Marcel Marceau mime: but then I read the article on the Internet.

I had, however, just read Richard Millet's little diatribe, *Désenchantement de la littérature* (Paris: Gallimard, 2007), which was much harsher on French culture: "I gradually came to realize that I was living in a country that is dead," said Richard Millet in an interview, before specifying that what was dead was "France as a universal literary nation."[5] There is nothing so definitive in Donald Morrison, but it is true that Richard Millet had also wounded some sensibilities and had been treated, if not as contemptibly anti-French, at least as a filthy reactionary.

Maryvonne de Saint-Pulgent – less cantankerous, more reasonable, and thus more redoubtable – a member of the Conseil d'État, and a former director of heritage at the Ministry of Culture, had just pointed out in a lecture that French culture, the traditional attribute of national power from the Ancien Régime to the Great War, and then a substitute for national power, had now lost even that consoling role. "Our services of cultural activity abroad," she claimed, "have developed in tandem with the decline of French economic and military power that ensued from the two world wars."[6] This, in her view, explained why national pride has these days taken refuge in the defense of culture, with the result that "any attack on French artistic renown is registered by public opinion as a threat to the nation itself." Resignedly, she did still acknowledge "the indisputable falling off of French cultural influence, which is now more regional than global."

But Richard Millet and Maryvonne de Saint-Pulgent were not alone, far from it: essays on French decline constitute a genre that has been in rude health in Paris for several years. Economic decline, industrial decline, diplomatic decline, cultural decline, literary decline: there's a decline to suit every taste. Even if we set aside the bestsellers by Nicolas Baverez, *Les trente piteuses* (Paris: Flammarion, 1997) and *La France qui tombe – un constat clinique du déclin français* (Paris: Perrin, 2003) – works that were soon superseded thanks to the speed at which current reality keeps changing – cries of alarm on the French malaise in culture and literature have proliferated since *L'État culturel – Essai sur une religion moderne* by Marc Fumaroli (Paris: de Fallois, 1991), followed by *La Comédie de la culture* by Michel Schneider (Paris: Seuil, 1993). Both authors gave a good dressing-down to the slide into demagogy in the cultural politics of France under the reign of Jack Lang: "creation by all" had replaced "culture for all." In fact, some twenty years ago, Marc Fumaroli and Michel Schneider, with others such as Alain Finkielkraut in *La Défaite de la pensée* (Paris: Gallimard, 1987; translated by Dennis O'Keefe as *The Undoing of Thought*, London: Claridge, 1988) had already pointed to the stagnation in French culture – people were reading less and going to high-cultural events less often, cultural diversity was all the rage, cultural artifacts were being commodified, and cultural consumerism had triumphed. These works linked this to the shift in ministerial policies from Malraux to Lang.

On an even more Franco-French note, people still remember the "Appeal Against the War on Intelligence" launched by *Les Inrockuptibles*[v] in March 2004 and signed by several intellectuals and cultural commentators against the government of Jean-Pierre Raffarin and the French Right, who were accused of showing "contempt for intelligence" and abandoning any cultural ambition, in other words of pursuing a "dead-dog, drift-along" policy in this regard (I was asked, but didn't sign this petition, since claiming to be on the side of intelligence seemed suspicious to me, and was too reminiscent of the "Parti de l'intelligence" launched by Henri Massis, the supporter of Maurras, in 1919).[vi]

Culture played barely any part in the presidential campaign of 2007. Neither Nicolas Sarkozy, nor Ségolène Royal, nor François Bayrou had much to say on the subject, even if several publications had insisted on the crisis in cultural policy in autumn 2006, including *Les Dérèglements de l'exception culturelle* by Françoise Benhamou (Seuil) and a dossier of the review *Le Débat* (November-December 2006). This dossier, entitled "Quelle politique pour la culture? [What policy for culture?]" brought together the responses of Jack Lang, Marc Fumaroli, Maryvonne de Saint-Pulgent, and Philippe Urfalino to a text by the sociologist of culture Nathalie Heinich attacking "cultural intermediaries," civil servants and other public agents, "all-powerful and lacking in any responsibility," who operated as a clique and failed to recognize artistic production in its full diversity.

Ever since, the works have continued to pour out: they include *Crises dans la culture française* by Antoine de Baecque (Bayard, 2008), *Le grand dégoût culturel* by Alain Brossat (Seuil, 2008), and *La Grande Déculturation* by Renaud Camus (Fayard, 2008). Whether they come from the left or the right, they all indulge in the same familiar refrain: "a decline in cultural practices," "a failure of cultural democratization," a "cultural fracture," a "cultural ghetto."[7] Or, more insidiously, the end of "the predominance of a properly 'French' culture in an increasingly intermixed society." Or indeed, concerning French influence abroad: a "cultural identity in pieces," a "decline in translations," the "collapse of French in European institutions and international organizations," and the "deterioration in the teaching of French abroad."[8] When it became known in March 2008 that France would be represented in the Eurovision Song Contest by a song in English, *Divine*, by Sébastien Tellier, members of the

French Parliament and the Secretary of State responsible for Francophone affairs expressed their surprise, but their anger soon subsided since it wasn't the only example of this kind of thing, and the evening went off at the end of May without making any waves – and without giving the French song a prize.[9]

One immediate consequence of the decline of the teaching of French throughout the world is the fact that the number of foreign students in France is also crumbling: in 2005 there were 250,000 (as in 1985), after dropping to 130,000 in 1997–1998. And in particular – figures that complete the dire picture painted by Donald Morrison – in a global market for knowledge and training that continues to expand, France takes in only 9 percent of students pursuing a higher education outside their own countries. This is far behind the United States (30 percent), but also behind the United Kingdom (14 percent), Germany (12 percent) and Australia (10 percent).[10]

As far as the art market goes, Donald Morrison pointed to the low esteem in which the French plastic arts are held. There was nothing new under the sun here for anyone who still remembered a glum article by Philippe Dagen in 2001, "Le lent effacement de l'art français sur la scène mondiale"[11] summarizing a report commissioned by the Ministry of Foreign Affairs from a sociologist on the place occupied by French artists on the international scene. In the view of Alain Quemin, the expert consulted by the Ministry, "contemporary French artists are very poorly represented in the permanent collections of the major international cultural institutions – which are, indeed, characterized by a very high concentration of the nationalities exhibited (and this phenomenon essentially benefits two countries, Germany and, above all, the United States) – and even in their temporary exhibitions. Not only that: the paucity is all the more marked the more recent the period is." In short, things weren't going well; they were even getting worse. The same verdict was reached on the representation of French artists at international art fairs and public sales. Philippe Dagen concluded: "In short, if we

95

look at the figures, contemporary French art finds itself in fourth place, equal with Italian art, in a situation completely dominated by the duo United States/Germany, which in itself constitutes at least two-thirds of the market and the contemporary scene. Great Britain [. . .], although unable to rival the giants, maintains its honourable third place." And he pointed out – as Fumaroli, Schneider, and the others had done – the negative effects of state policy, which turns culture into a public service: "nineteen French galleries were subsidized so they could take part in the Basel Fair 2000 – a detail that is already itself a handicap in the eyes of the market – and, at their exhibition stands as well as in the catalogue, they exhibited more foreign than French artists."

You won't find anything crueller in Donald Morrison, except that the situation has worsened since 2001. In any case, commenting on the results of the last Kunst Kompass, Alain Quemin soberly took up the cudgels again in November 2007: "Announcing a rescue plan for the French art market, Christine Albanel acknowledged that 'its decline was undeniable.' This statement by the Minister for Culture is something of an understatement."[12]

As for literature, each season brings with it a new and grim little survey: *L'Adieu à la littérature* by William Marx (Minuit, 2005), *Contre Saint Proust, ou la fin de la littérature* by Dominique Maingueneau (Belin, 2006), or *La littérature en péril* by Tzvetan Todorov (Flammarion, 2007), not to mention Richard Millet, Alain Finkielkraut, Renaud Camus . . . They all repeat the idea – echoed by Donald Morrison – that the formalist and nihilistic theorizing of the 1960s and 1970s has sterilized the French novel, as if French literature weren't big enough to die all by itself and as if theory, like the quartermaster's stores, hadn't always tagged along behind.

Thus, we French have a specialty–cultural lamentation, a bewailing over our decline – since I can't see anything similar outside France. It's reminiscent of Chateaubriand, the "futile Cassandra," as he cried in the Chamber of Peers on August 7, 1830, when he refused to swear the oath of loyalty to

Louis-Philippe. And this can produce some fine poetry, such as Baudelaire's lines in the second *Spleen* poem:

An old sphinx ignored by the careless world,
Forgotten on the map, and whose wild moods
Sing to the sun's rays only when it sets.

We have long cultivated a French tradition of prophets of disaster and hired mourners of culture. The undoing of thought is our familiar muse of morose delectation. We bewail the bankruptcy of high culture, the failure of the democratization of the arts, the end of humanism, the ruin of education, the invasion of mass culture, and the entertainment industry. No country is as fascinated as is ours by the decline of its language. Everyone, including the English-speaking countries, seems exposed to the same cultural precariousness when faced with the domination of the new lingua franca based on English, the power of culture industries across the world, and the demands that different cultures and communities be respected. However, this whole poetry of decadence can be found neither among our European neighbors nor among our American friends.

But lay off my pal![vii] This poetry constituted our greatness, it was our monopoly, and it must remain so. May the swan-song be our last privilege! In our wretchedness, we claim the greatness of proclaiming our own end ourselves! Donald Morrison is telling us nothing we didn't already know, nothing that countless articles, broadcasts, and essays have not been remorselessly repeating to us for nearly thirty years. The way we continue to put May '68 on trial is itself a genre in which our national complacency exercises itself. We can say everything when at home among ourselves but, as with family secrets, the minute an outsider thinks he can give us lessons, when the prophecy of disaster comes from outside, and – even worse – from an America with which we have a love-hate relationship, and which is perceived as our sole rival when it comes to universalist ambitions, then the chauvinistic or jingoistic reaction will be intense. People throng together to set up a safety cordon: their persecution complex hectically transforms every skeptic into an enemy of the French.

After all, let's not spit into our own soup. This quasi-unanimous reaction might have its good side, as when the first Shanghai list of the best world universities was published in 2003. There were many of us, on all sides, who had for years been denouncing the dreadful state of French universities, the lack of means at their disposal and the mediocrity of their ambitions. This disclosure, in a foreign source, of the national clobbering we had taken was essential if public opinion and the political class were finally to realize that reform was urgently necessary. When we French people told each other that the emperor had no clothes, it seemed like a turn of speech. Nobody believed us, and maybe we didn't really believe it ourselves, following the old doctrine of the double truth: the announcement of French decline, when peddled among ourselves, stems partly from a magical style of thinking that hopes to conjure away the effects of this decline by pointing a finger at it. In all the elegies for culture published in France each year, we have been crying "Wolf!" so loud and so long that the day when the wolf finally enters the house of culture, nobody wants to know.

But Donald Morrison's charge sheet has little chance of producing the same effect as the Shanghai list of universities. To begin with, if the latter hurt us so much, it was because it disrespected not only our poor universities, but also the jewels in the crown, those superb *grandes écoles* which select the élite of our decision-makers and yet didn't come out of the evaluation any better. Then, this list came just after the European Council in Lisbon, which in 2000 had set the European Union the objective of becoming "the most competitive and most dynamic knowledge economy in the world between now and 2010." There was nothing of the kind for culture: Europe did not measure culture's contribution to economic activity, and our political and financial élites did not grasp the fact that it was a condition of private and public success. After a few weeks of ritual dance, the fever abated. Everyone blamed the thermometer instead of taking the malady seriously, and trotted back to their own preoccupations. If Donald Morrison's article had been published in the Hong Kong *South China Morning Post*, and not in an American magazine, perhaps it would have had a bigger effect in the long term.

3.

At the risk of hurting our feelings, Donald Morrison puts us firmly back in our place: we are a middle-ranking cultural power on the world scale, as suits our status as a middle-ranking economic power. French, spoken by some 80 million speakers as mother tongue and by 128 million speakers as second or third language, is now only the eighth or even twelfth language in the world,[13] as our nominal GDP is sixth in the world in overall size, but seventeenth on a per capita basis. Now we have long claimed that economic and cultural power did not go together, and that – at least as far as France was concerned – the historic eminence of its culture magnified its international influence. *Quand l'Europe parlait français* (de Fallois, 2001) is the title of a book by Marc Fumaroli: it means "when Europe spoke French," and was his proud way of describing the Age of Enlightenment in counterpoint to his dark musings in *État culturel*. French remained the universal language of diplomacy until the Treaty of Versailles. While still an official language in international organizations, French is increasingly yielding to English, not only in the U.N. and the W.T.O., but also in European bodies.[14] On the internet, finally, French is struggling to maintain its presence, including on the sites of French businesses in which the state is a shareholder, such as the electronics firm Thalès or the aircraft construction company Airbus.

The French seem to have believed for a long time that their culture would preserve all its international prerogatives in spite of the fading prestige of their country and even of their language throughout the world. In 2007, the autumn music season in New York was mainly French, featuring Natalie Dessay, Pierre Boulez, and Pierre-Laurent Aimard. And in spring 2008, we could also congratulate ourselves on the fact that the museum and gallery season had a very French flavor, with two exceptional exhibitions at the Metropolitan Museum, of a highly impressive kind rarely found in the same museum: one of the works of Poussin and the other of Courbet. But I am not altogether convinced by this type of argument, which has more to do with cultural heritage than with so-called living culture. A third exhibition in the Metropolitan Museum, just as remarkable, brought together for display the grisailles of Jasper Johns: it's difficult to see which contemporary French artist could vie with him.

Four years ago, the annual translation prize awarded by the French-American Foundation (I have been on the jury for twelve years now) was given to the translator of *Silbermann* by Jacques de Lacretelle, a slim but powerful narrative from 1922 on the way a schoolboy at the turn of the century first encountered anti-Semitism. We made this choice not for lack of any other careful translations, but because there were no contemporary works among the translations submitted to the jury that were felt to be substantial enough. Two years ago, in 2006, we awarded the prize to the translation of Irène Némirovsky's *Suite française*: this was something of an endorsement of the book's success, since this posthumous novel had been given the Prix Renaudot in 2004, and the death of the author in Auschwitz in 1942, as well as the adventures of the manuscript, rediscovered after sixty years, promised that the book would touch its American readers (for 102 weeks it appeared on the *New York Times* list of bestsellers). I wasn't all that keen on the work – it is written in a rather dated style – but out of the 700 to 800 new French novels on sale in the bookshops every autumn, at the start of each new literary season, fewer than a dozen will be translated in the United States, most of them by university presses that have no commercial gain in view, thanks to subsidies from the National Book Center, the cultural services of the French Embassy, or the Florence Gould Foundation; and one may well wonder why it is these books that are chosen rather than others. Practically every year, we find ourselves faced with the same dilemma, as we are forced to decide between a new translation of Balzac, Stendhal, or Proust and that of a relatively unimportant contemporary novel. Fortunately, this year, 2008, *Ravel* by Jean Echenoz helped us out of our quandary: it is the seventh of his novels to be translated into English, and the third by the same publisher; he has a faithful readership, and he has lived up to their expectations on several occasions.

The other arts are not exported with any more success, neither film (which is doing quite well in metropolitan France itself), nor music, nor painting. Of course, Marion Cotillard won the 2008 Oscar for best actress for her performance in the role of Édith Piaf in *La Môme – La Vie en rose* in English; she was only the second French actress (after Simone Signoret) to win a Hollywood statuette in this category, the second actress (after Sophia Loren) to be given a prize for a performance in a language other than English, and the first to be crowned for a role in French. It is true that her reputation was soon tarnished by the discovery of conspiracy-theory-type remarks she made in February 2007 questioning the circumstances of the attacks of September 11. Then, for the first time since 1987, the Palme d'Or of the Cannes Festival was awarded to a French film, *Entre les murs* (*The Class*) by Laurent Cantet, a very politically correct docu-drama on diversity in schools. Also in spring 2008, Jean Nouvel won the Pritzker Prize for architecture, only the second Frenchman to be recognized in this way since the award was created in 1979. And the Nobel Prize for Literature was awarded to J. M. G. Le Clézio in autumn 2008, after the secretary of the Swedish Academy had judged American literature to be "too isolated, too insular."

These awards do not mean much, and contemporary French literature and philosophy have little to pride themselves on in this domain, whereas they had travelled well until recently. In 2008, Muriel Barbery, author of *L'Élégance du hérisson* (2006, translated as *The Elegance of the Hedgehog* by Alison Anderson), was the top French author in the list of most-read writers in Europe, in sixth place, thanks mostly to her sales in France, ahead of Anna Gavalda (twelfth), and Le Clézio (fifteenth, thanks to the Nobel Prize). Ever since the generation of "modern classics" born around 1870 – Gide, Valéry, Proust, and Claudel, then Péguy, Colette, and various others – French creativity has not faltered. Existentialism, the *nouveau roman*, structuralism, and poststructuralism have followed one another, often being first recognized abroad (especially in the United States) before returning to France with added prestige thanks to this detour. A received idea claims that Theory was the last avant-garde of Old World origin, after which the New World took over, just as the art market had moved from Paris to New York thanks to World War II.

Some argue that French literature is not the only one to have gone into retreat, and other European literatures are no better off in the global market – they too are going through a bad patch. People take whatever consolation they can, and it is not certain that this judgment is correct. For a long time, no French novel has been as successful as the German book *The Reader* by Bernhard Schlink,[15] selected for Oprah Winfrey's book club, the first German novel to take the number one spot on the *New York Times* bestseller lists. At the same time, the work of W. G. Sebald, in particular *The Emigrants*[16] and *Austerlitz*,[17] was a revelation that, once again, happened first in the United States before being confirmed elsewhere, especially in France.

These are just a few examples, and commercial success does not prove artistic value – as Maurice Druon and Olivier Poivre d'Arvor did not fail to remind an American journalist accused of confusing art and money – but they do suggest that there is something unusual about the dearth of good French works. Of course, there is nothing to say that it will last. The situation might change overnight. *The Diving Bell and the Butterfly* (Robert Laffont, 1997), not a novel but the story of the life and death of Jean-Dominique Bauby who, following a stroke, was left unable to move anything but one of his eyelids, and communicated with the world in this way, was a great success in American translation, and was filmed by Julian Schnabel in 2007 with Mathieu Amalric – a great transatlantic success.

In short, the influence of French culture abroad is now consistent with the geopolitical heft of France in the world, and with its foreign trade. Indeed, culture contributes to the deficit in our trade balance since, in a historic reversal of trends, we import many more cultural products than we export.[18] This relegation to second division probably does not concern France alone, but it hits us especially hard because the new balance between the various cultures on the world stage has a mechanical result: as the cultural influence of France wanes, that of some of its European neighbors, such as Italy and Spain, increases, and we watch as our former cultural pre-eminence shrinks and shrinks like a pair of Levis.

With globalization, it seems that national cultures cannot automatically claim international status. Moreover, are cultures still national? Is Louise Bourgeois, who has lived in New York for over seventy years, a French artist? And there are more and more people like Louise Bourgeois in the world – French expatriate artists, creating their oeuvres in New York, London, Berlin, or Tokyo, and enjoying success, more than if they had remained in Paris. The words "French culture," if they still mean anything at all, no longer have the same meaning as before. But France (where, more than anywhere else, culture and nation continue to share an identity in people's minds) is more affected than other countries by the current dispersal of national cultures in the global network of all community-based cultures. This situation, once again, is perhaps not irreversible, but it is one of the reasons for the malaise that affects us especially.

4.

Donald Morrison, following a by now well-established idea, tends to explain the crisis in contemporary French culture by the way it is paid for out of the state budget and transformed into a public service. This was the idea put forward by Marc Fumaroli in *L'État culturel* and widely adopted since. French culture is declining, he says, not in spite of but because of a disproportionate public budget (3 billion euros in 2007 just for the Department of Culture; in real terms, a tenfold increase in subsidies since 1959; 22,000 employees in 2007, which is the equivalent of 30 percent of the jobs in the Department of Justice; direct public aid amounting to 208 euros per capita, as against 120 in the United Kingdom and a few dollars in the United States). France has a drip-fed culture, heavily subsidized by the state and by regional and municipal authorities, a "cultural welfare state" in the words of Dominique Schnapper,[19] but – as a direct consequence – one that arouses no echoes outside France. State culture discourages the private initiative, competition, and emulation required in the marketplace of ideas and talent. Thus public subsidies enable French creativity to scrape along at home without having to face the global market.

The best example, or so it is claimed, is French cinema: being the second largest cinema worldwide after Hollywood, it survives better than the film industry in other countries of the European Union. But French films, whether big-budget or low-budget, are mainly designed for the home market and television, and only one in ten of them ever earns a sum worth mentioning from being exported, even in Francophone countries (fewer than 50 percent of French films are still exportable to Belgium, and fewer than 25 percent to Canada), an especially disappointing result if we remember that, given the historical role of the Cannes Festival, French exporters control 80 percent of the global market for *films d'auteur*.

In March 2008, the Club of the 13 – an independent group of filmmakers gathered around the director Pascale Ferran – released an even more alarming report questioning the policy of the National Center for Cinematography and the Ministry: they pointed to declining quality, increasing polarization between large and small budgets, nonrenewal of contracts for talented people, overmerchandising, and a counterproductive support system:

> the overabundance of French production and the poor quality of much of it are detrimental to the marketing of French films that would be most successful internationally. [. . .] Twenty years ago, a foreigner would go to see a "French movie" because this represented, consciously or not, a cultural act with its own specific identity. Unfortunately, this is no longer the case today.[20]

There are exceptions, but despite successes in the United States such as *La Vie en rose* (whose popularity owed more to the Piaf myth than to the genius of its director Olivier Dahan), overall, the share of French films abroad is in decline.

Typical of a conception of culture as a public service is the system of solidarity whereby the entire society supports those who work in the performing arts. This system, though it was reformed in 2003, is unique in the world: foreigners find it perplexing. While American actors are part of a free-market system and top up their earnings (or simply earn a living) as waiters – they do occasional work, they moonlight, though most of their income can come from this moonlighting – their French counterparts are still covered by unemployment insurance for 8 months if they cannot find employment after working for 507 hours during the previous 10 months. This is enough to convince Donald Morrison and many other observers that it is the grants, accrued benefits, and safety nets that are hindering artistic production in France.

Piaf and Némirovsky, Poussin and Courbet, or even Boulez: classic French culture is still beautiful despite its age, but it is living culture and artistic creativity that the French Ministry is accused of stifling with its subsidies. This argument may attract the most convinced French free-marketeers, but it is not necessarily irrefutable. First, there is nothing more complicated than calculating the consolidated budget for culture in France, or anywhere else in Europe. And the difficulty is even greater in the United States, where this budget includes not only federal funding as well as that of states and cities, but where it rests mainly on tax exemption for noncommercial activities, which are deemed to include nonprofit cultural enterprises (as well as schools and universities). This allows them simultaneously to pay no taxes and to reap donations that, themselves, benefit from tax deductions. Culture in the United States is sponsored by a tax shortfall which does not seem significantly lower than French public spending on culture per capita, according to Frédéric Martel in his excellent book, *De la culture en Amérique* (Gallimard, 2006).

Yet, although the amount of United States' spending is close to the French budget, there is still a considerable advantage: thanks to reliance on tax exemption, the public administration of culture is reduced to next to nothing, thus saving American artistic life from the formatting of a national cultural policy. People will doubtless object that the State Department and the CIA contributed greatly to the promotion of abstract expressionism in Europe in the early days of the Cold War, as Serge Guilbaut showed in an investigation into the transfer of the art market from Paris to New York after 1945.[21] And the clumsy interventions of the National Endowment for the Arts (NEA), despite its paltry budget, were instrumental in triggering and aggravating the "culture wars" in the United States in the late 1980s, when the allegedly pornographic photos of Robert Mapplethorpe or the sacrilegious montages of Andres Serrano caused a storm. On the other hand, while the United States manages without a public arts administration and therefore does not have a state cultural policy, this still comes down to transferring responsibility for this administration to other cultural intermediaries, mainly foundations. Yet these foundations, which have become entangled in ever more bureaucracy over the years, and the increasing complexity of tax law, are now almost as ponderous as the French civil service.

And United States private foundations, over the last thirty years, have pursued a cultural policy, or indeed a cultural revolution, that is just as much determined by ideology as the French Ministry of Culture. In France, in accordance with the schematic view now current, the censors of the contemporary "cultural whole" claim that it was the ministry of Jack Lang which made the shift from the republican democratization of élite culture (which was the aim of Malraux and his *maisons de la culture*) to cultural democracy as an acknowledgment of the equal legitimacy of various community-based cultures, or even of their equal value. But Frédéric Martel's work on American culture rightly reminds us – and from the point of view of the Franco-French debate, this is, in my opinion, his greatest achievement – that the ideology of cultural diversity had already replaced that of the democratization of culture in the United States before 1981, notably at the Ford Foundation, which began to shift its ground in the late 1960s. The presidency of Jimmy Carter (1977–1981) was to confirm this trend by promoting communities – their empowerment, their pride, their rise to power – as the instruments of a different city policy, breaking with the Democratic program of federal intervention, from the New Deal of Franklin Roosevelt to the Great Society of Lyndon Johnson. Frédéric Martel demonstrates – at least this is the conclusion I draw from his analysis – that in 1981, France, despite May 1968 and all the social transgressiveness now imputed to it, lagged behind the United States, which was already encouraging the expression of cultural diversity by quite different means. And the wealthiest private foundations had now begun to subsidize generously not only the democratization of the institutions of high culture – access to social strata that had not inherited the habit of going to museums and libraries, operas and orchestra concerts, the theaters and the ballet – but also the practices of minority cultures, especially in black neighborhoods and the ghettos of big cities.

In short, it appears that only after 1981 did France's cultural policy catch up with the United States in its shift to cultural diversity and the equal dignity of cultures. Jack Lang was thus going along with a broad social movement, after a period in which a string of short-lived ministers from 1969 to 1981, under the presidencies of Georges Pompidou and Valéry Giscard d'Estaing, had merely managed affairs on a day-to-day basis. Indeed, Jacques Duhamel, minister under

Trappings of Greatness

Pompidou from 1971 to 1973, had already changed the focus of the work of the ministry, emphasizing the "cultural practices" of different social groups and the "original cultural life" of the country. In the same years (the 1970s and 1980s), West Germany, without any Federal Ministry of Culture but with funding for culture based on the principle of subsidiarity (in which the regions and the federal government complete the cultural projects financed by the municipalities) also shifted towards the recognition of community-based and alternative cultures. First in the municipalities and the *Länder* ruled by the SPD and the Greens, "culture from below" was promoted by sociocultural programs and neighborhood cultural centers, then, under the Christian Democrat Chancellor Helmut Kohl, "socioculture" was incorporated into federal government policy.[22] Indeed, the convergence of European cultural policies was remarkable in the 1980s, in France, Germany, and the United Kingdom, whatever the political complexion of the government in power.

Should we conclude that there was nothing original about the French cultural revolution of the 1980s? Certainly not; but focusing on the gap between Malraux and Lang means ignoring the guilt of the élite (the idea of the "duty of repentance" had not yet emerged) and the failure of democratization (the standstill in what was not yet called "social mobility") which transformed cultural policies everywhere, both private and public, and imposed cultural diversity. In France, indeed, this slogan did not establish itself until the late 1990s, later than elsewhere.

Previously, France had advocated the "cultural exception," summed up by Jacques Delors before the GATT negotiations in 1993 in a striking phrase: "Culture is not a commodity like any other." France, through the European Commission, then managed to get this principle accepted, preserving the French right to impose quotas against the "invasion" of American films and broadcasts, and the opportunity to pursue policies of national and community-based aid. Although this position was not shared in Europe, the Commission did not open the sector of the broadcasting industries up to competition. But nothing was settled, and at the WTO negotiations in Seattle in 1999, the Commission replaced the "cultural exception," with its overdefensive and protectionist feel, with the principle of "cultural diversity," in order to contrast the spirit of free competition with its letter, in other words the de facto monopoly of Hollywood. Cultural diversity, consistent with the multiculturalism of identity politics, became the doctrine of the European Union in cultural matters, and France conformed to it, albeit reluctantly.

It is true that cultural diversity might well be the last trick of the United States' entertainment industries to perpetuate their global monopoly. While in France, the cultural diversity introduced in the wake of the United States and promoted by Jack Lang – one of whose first acts in 1981 was to boycott the Festival of American Cinema at Deauville – proved to be defensive, on the other side of the Atlantic, cultural diversity has become a hot seller on the international market. It is in the United States that much of the Latin music played in Latin America, including Cuba as well as in Spain and Portugal, is produced: multiculturalism, like Benetton ads, sells.

This could suggest that Bernard-Henri Lévy was right when, in an opinion piece in the *Guardian*, he interpreted Donald Morrison's cry of alarm with regard to French culture as the symptom of an anxiety on the part of Americans about the future of their own culture when faced with multiculturalism and miscegenation. So he answered tit-for-tat: "France as metaphor for America. Anti-French hostility as a displaced form of panic which dare not speak its name."[23] So far, it seems that the old culture has resisted the rise of cultural diversity in the United States pretty well, and that, after the "culture wars" of the late 1980s and the disputes over the canon in universities – for or against replacing Saint Augustine's *Confessions* as a first-year text with *I, Rigoberta Menchu: An Indian Woman in Guatemala* – there is room for everything, including any old thing, on the American cultural and academic market. On the one hand, we have the "business as usual" of the civic humanities and the Three

Tenors; on the other, postcolonialism and globalization blowing in every wind.

But, the other day, I took two women friends to the Salle Pleyel for a Baroque recital. They had just arrived from New York. They pointed out – I no longer notice, as I come and go so often – how much younger and more diverse, more colorful, the audience was than at Carnegie Hall or the New York Philharmonic. European culture that American philanthropy once strove to democratize is becoming a culture for old people. This is encouraging, since there are more and more old people – or "senior citizens," as the euphemism in vogue has it – but it is also worrying. After all, there is no guarantee that the "young adults" of today, following another circumlocution in fashion, will use their tax-exempt donations to finance European culture once they're getting on a bit. If ABC, CBS, and NBC, the historic channels, have reasons to worry about their future, given that the modes of cultural consumption of young Americans, all hooked on the Internet, are changing, then so – and to an even greater degree – do the Met, MoMA, or the Santa Fe Festival of Chamber Music.

5.

Maurice Druon responded to the indictment of Donald Morrison in *Le Figaro* by denouncing the typically American confusion between culture and entertainment: "Culture is not determined by the box office takings of the week. Culture exerts its influence over time. Sartre and Malraux are still our contemporaries." Maurice Druon – since deceased – was playing his former role as Pompidou's Minister of Cultural Affairs and former permanent secretary of the French Academy, defending France as "the land of culture for centuries past and, let us hope, for centuries to come."[24] *Le Figaro* illustrated his opinion piece with a gallery of recent French successes throughout the world: painting, philosophy, cinema, and architecture, but little literature and a great deal of equestrian theater.

In his "Letter to our American friends," the director of Culturesfrance, Olivier Poivre d'Arvor, responded by defending the protective measures (such as quotas for pop songs), and justifying the new official doctrine of cultural diversity – in short, certifying the good health of French culture and the vigor of its reception abroad.[25] Then he distributed a hundred thousand copies of two bilingual (French-English and French-Spanish) booklets imitating the cover of *Time* and identifying three hundred French creative artists whose "talents transcend borders": Brigitte Bardot, Yannick Noah, Vanessa Paradis, and Joël Robuchon ... He too was in his role as patron of the operator – the heir, since 2006, of the former Association française d'action artistique (AFAA) and Association pour la diffusion de la pensée française (ADPF) – to which the Ministry of Foreign Affairs and the Ministry of Culture delegate their international cultural exchanges. The Culturesfrance association, acting on behalf of the State, is not really independent of it, since it obtains over 80 percent of its budget of 29 million euros (in 2007) from it, and struggles to increase the share from its other resources, particularly sponsorship (less than 5 percent). Through the voices of Maurice Druon and Olivier Poivre d'Arvor, France was expressing itself quasi-officially.

But in the list of awards bestowed on French culture drawn up by the director of Culturesfrance, we find, mixed up together rather as in the tableau presented in *Le Figaro*, high and low, élite culture and entertainment, art and *de luxe* commodities, and poetry and gastronomy. Neither Culturesfrance, nor the Foreign Ministry which sets its objectives and its means, appears to have a clear sense of mission, or knows where to turn to promote French culture abroad.

The actions of Culturesfrance are very diverse and quite heterogeneous, without its priorities emerging: cultural interventions abroad, but also the hosting in France of foreign artists, particularly the promotion of the cultures of our former colonies; the dissemination of French arts and culture in most areas and in at least eighty countries every year, but also activities encouraging the international recognition of contemporary artistic production in poorer regions and countries, including support for the big African exhibitions of contemporary art. Despite the display of these good intentions, the interventions are actually highly concentrated in Europe and North America (more than half their number), although this figure is not openly admitted. The operator finances the tours of variety artists to the United States and Canada, or Parisian art galleries participating in the major international fairs in Basel, Cologne, Chicago, or New York, even if they put on show only a minority of French artists. Reading the record of one year of Culturesfrance's activities across the world – Les Talens Lyriques (Baroque music) in Paraguay, Molière's *Les Fourberies de Scapin* (Comédie-Française) in Central Europe, Accrorap (hip-hop) in Panama, Les Plasticiens Volants (street art) in the Philippines, and so on – it is difficult to resist the impression of a dispersion of activity and a scattering of small amounts of finance, despite the ambitious goals announced in the statutes. Indeed, the program seems to choose between the requests from some hundred and fifty French cultural services abroad rather than implementing its own strategic guidelines.

Over the past thirty years, as I have observed from New York France's cultural activity abroad, it is its variations, uncertainties, and inconsistencies that strike me most. There is hesitation as to the type of action to support, the people involved change course more often than government, and priorities are constantly modified without prior assessment of the methods eventually abandoned. Instead of long-term actions, patient and subterranean, but less visible and too discreet, people tend to prefer media fireworks, dazzling but expensive, which will make it possible for a splendid dossier of local press cuttings to be assembled and sent, with a great fanfare, to Paris, in self-justification. But what will be left tomorrow, once the footlights are extinguished? A whole line-up of writers is brought together, at great expense, for a panel discussion in front of a sparse audience – but their books will not be translated in any greater quantities, or if some of them are, they will be those of authors who had already been translated in the past without any help from the embassy. In spring 2008, Culturesfrance hoped to organize, for October 2008, the first "French Fiction Festival in New York" which, as well as awarding a literary prize to one of some seven hundred French novels published in the autumn, would have welcomed a dozen writers – including Pascal Quignard, Michel Houellebecq, Yasmina Rza, Marie N'Diaye, Julia Kristeva, Édouard Glissant, Maryse Condé, Assia Djebar, Jean Echenoz, and Alain Mabanckou – who had all been previously translated, were often invited to American universities, and were as familiar as could be in the French Institutes: not one of them needed any public intervention to travel. The project fell through, for lack of agreement with the New York Public Library, which was meant to host it but which – in striking evidence of the clash of two cultural logics – did not accept the role of silent partner that Culturesfrance wished it to take in the selecting of participants. A smaller-scale meeting, the Festival of New French Writing, was held in conquered territory, at New York University, in February 2009. Similarly, aid is given to galleries that display French artists, but they favor those who were already in their catalogues, since no subsidy can ever change the laws of a market that has its own rationality.

With the rise of the Ministry of Culture, the cultural domain took precedence over the educational in activities outside France. Among the cultural attachés and counsellors, as well as the staff seconded to French Institutes, teachers have given way to coordinators. The high-level academic network created by the Third Republic, a network affecting thousands of students, with university chairs at Oxford, Cambridge, and Manchester, Istanbul and Beirut, Jerusalem, Cairo and Alexandria, Athens and Thessaloniki, Sao Paulo, and (of course) in the Maghreb and sub-Saharan Africa (Dakar, Abidjan, Cotonou, Yaoundé . . .), has been dismantled, even if, as in Egypt, ruinously expensive (and unsuccessful) French and

Trappings of Greatness

Francophone universities have been rebuilt. Of course, we are no longer living in the time of "missionaries," as the French Foreign Ministry continues to call the representatives of French culture that it sends abroad; and in our former colonies, people often prefer to deal with Belgian and Canadian voluntary workers. But the Agence Universitaire de la Francophonie, comprising hundreds of universities in over seventy countries, which derive more than 80 percent of their budgets from France, is struggling to take up the challenge of keeping the French language alive throughout the world.

Many rich French Institute libraries have been dispersed to make room for media libraries *cum* cafeterias. During the year, when the central government freezes funds on the orders of the Budget Ministry, services start by cutting into scholarships in France because this is what is more fungible. It so happens that twenty or thirty years later on, former holders of French government scholarships turn out to be the best ambassadors for French culture throughout the world, in Cairo or Jerusalem, Kyoto or Buenos Aires. The Ministry of Foreign Affairs does not have a directory of its former scholars, so it is not possible to use these "alumni" of France, to mobilize them in defense of French culture, perhaps even to ask them to make a donation. And yet, in the course of my travels, I have encountered many of these former scholars – a Zeev Sternhell, a Yoshio Abe, an Ibrahim Rugova – who have become great teachers of literature, history, or political science, or diplomats and politicians, who feel a deep debt to France and who would honor it with their gratitude if they were asked.

As an academic by temperament, I tend to think that the most beneficial actions of the French cultural services are the most patient ones, since they aim at the long term (rather than assembling a "pressbook"), starting with the support given to the teaching of French in high schools or even at the primary level. Therein, essentially, lies the future of French culture. But no missionary will derive any glory from having ensured that a small bilingual school gains one more teacher, compared to the immediate gratification of organizing and publicizing a dance festival.

The fact of the matter is that France no longer knows how to promote its language and culture in the world. People just grope around. The Villa Médicis was in the news in spring 2008 due to the controversial appointment of its director (the director of Culturesfrance was also dragged into this controversy, before a high-flying coordinator – now Minister of Culture – won this plum job). The Villa Médicis is an establishment with an ambiguous mission. Traditionally, it was the Academy of French artists in residence in Rome – artists and musicians, most recently writers – but is now also a cultural institute for the Italian public. But it fulfils neither of its functions satisfactorily: artists would probably receive a better introduction to contemporary art outside Rome, or in a "Villa Médicis Outside the Walls" (there is one, actually, managed by Culturesfrance), and Italians would probably attend more events at a full-fledged French Institute. As was noted in a parliamentary report of 2001 produced by the Senator for the Aube and member of the right-wing Union for a Popular Movement (UMP), Yann Gaillard, the Academy of France in Rome, which "has no longer any tradition to transmit," "brings together prizewinners without any interests in common" and "at the expense of the French Republic invites artists – in the broadest sense of the word – to a capital that is not, and has not been for a long time, an important center of artistic production." (Imagine the storm in a teacup there would be if an Italian senator had the gall to consign Paris to history this casually!) In short, "does the Villa Médicis, a superb container, still have any contents?"[26]

If it did not exist, would we set it up nowadays? If Colbert had not founded it and Napoleon not reestablished it, would anyone hesitate to reform it, or abolish it altogether? The Senator (UMP) of the Haute-Loire, Adrien Gouteyron, asked these reasonable questions at the height of the debate on the management of the Villa.[27] But there are so many of these venerable French institutions that would not withstand the same critical test: our *grandes écoles*, our state bodies, and (why not?) the Institut de France itself, our five academies and their academicians. It is true that, in France, we are not in the habit of abolishing anything. We invent new institutions rather than adapting or suppressing the old ones. The many avatars of the University (the Collège de France, the École Pratique, the CNRS, the IUF, the PRES, the RTRA, and other acronyms)[viii] were each created to make up for the shortcomings of the university system, instead of reforming it. From the outside, this costly piling up of institutions seems surprising. But they do have one advantage: a culture is made up of traditions, and France, a country of periodical revolutions, has not retained many of these traditions. Should we really get rid of the few idiosyncrasies that remain to us in order to look more European and international?

Nevertheless, people would like be sure that the budget for France's foreign cultural mission is being spent in the best possible manner, the most effective in the long term. Is a recently set up Bureau du Livre – nothing to do with Richelieu, Napoleon, or Rome – encouraging enough translations of French works to justify its budget being renewed year after year? Perhaps it outlives itself because the Ministry of Culture provides it with most of its budget, because it doesn't cost its publishers much (and they all club together for the rest), and thus it evades the constraints of bookkeeping? A recent audit conducted on the activity of Unifrance, the association subsidized by the Ministries of Foreign Affairs and Culture to promote French films abroad, has denounced its thinly dispersed activities and confessed to puzzlement about its actual effectiveness due to a "deficit in the setting of objectives, criteria and indicators for evaluation."[28]

It is difficult to get a clear idea of the total budget that France spends on its cultural activity abroad. According to a recent report by Senator Gouteyron, we spent over one billion euros in 2007 to promote our culture abroad: 35 percent of this was for "the largest cultural network in the world" and 21 percent for foreign broadcasting.[29] The Ministry of Foreign Affairs is the main contributor, but the Ministries of Culture,

Education, and Higher Education are also involved, not to mention the Ministry for Cooperation and French-Speaking Countries. Senator Gouteyron recommends "the end of the monopoly of the Quai d'Orsay [that is, the Foreign Ministry]" as it is "less an actor than a spectator" and the "value added" element of its cultural network "is not properly evaluated." The General Review of Public Policy (Révision générale des politiques publiques – RGPP), an overhaul intended to develop scenarios of reform for a more efficient and more economical administration, which, under the aegis of the Minister of the Budget, makes civil servants quake, should undertake this assessment. On the one hand, it proposes the "bringing together of all aspects of intellectual influence abroad under three operators: the Agency for the Teaching of French abroad, Culturesfrance, and a new operator responsible for international mobility." On the other hand, it suggests a "merger of services of cultural cooperation and cultural centers under a single label within one institution, with greater financial independence."[30] This will result in the increased accountability of both national operators and local institutions. But the RGPP proceeds more easily on a ministry-by-ministry basis, and inter-ministerial activities, or those that cut across different organizations, are even more difficult to optimize than others.

It would also be desirable to have a comparative assessment of France's cultural activities abroad and those of some of its neighbors, such as the United Kingdom or Germany. With the Goethe-Institut – whose sphere of influence was also reduced to 140 branches in 81 countries, with a budget of around 200 million euros, three-quarters of it from the Ministry of Foreign Affairs – and the DAAD (German Academic Exchange Service), which promotes exchanges of students, teachers, and researchers, Germany seems to have managed to contain its operating costs to increase its budget for real activities. Its combined 2007 budget for cultural activities abroad was 680 million euros. These funded activities remain more traditional or academic, less ambitious and media-based than those of France: they relate to language, art, and society, but also to general knowledge, including science and technology – and libraries are still called libraries.

As for France, it has, historically speaking, had two parallel networks: that of the Alliances Françaises, nearly five hundred of them around the globe, with 40 million euros from the ministry over and above their own resources, and some hundred and fifty French Institutes, which cost 100 million euros.[31] But are these figures themselves reliable?[32] One can never be sure what they leave out, for example whether expatriate or seconded staff members are counted. The RGPP envisages – and this is an old silly-season story – the merger of franchised Alliances Françaises and French Institutes. Why not, provided that this is not just an opportunity for the Ministry of Foreign Affairs to back out, but rather to optimize its cultural mission, reduce its structural costs and rebalance its activities in the countries in which it is found?[33]

6.

Basically, if Donald Morrison has offended us, it is because he has reminded us that the French arts really are increasingly isolated on the world stage. Some areas remain at the forefront, such as architecture or museography – as evidenced by the Louvre projects in Atlanta and Abu Dhabi and the controversy they have caused – while others lag behind, such as literature or the plastic arts. I repeat: despite some omissions and some exaggerations, this finding seems undeniable, and no chauvinistic or anti-American reflex will change a thing about it. So it is best to accept it, try to explain it, and attempt to remedy it.

As far as intellectual life and the movement of ideas, my own assessment would be less hesitant. Certainly, French thought is in a position of relative solitude in the global marketplace of ideas and talents, but our standard of measurement is an unusual yardstick that has lasted for years: a state of often affected and probably exaggerated excitement for a "French thought" identified with the Terror. We need merely recall that it was not in the departments of philosophy that fashionable French philosophers were long read on American campuses, and then in academia worldwide. Today, the French philosophers translated into English do not enjoy the same impact and no longer make the front cover of the *New York Times Magazine*: but this does not at all mean that their influence, more rarefied and insidious, is not ultimately more profound or enduring. Moreover, aloofness from a global market of ideas and talents increasingly modelled on the market of sports or show-biz may have advantages as well as disadvantages.

France is under-represented in the international network comprising the Society of Fellows, the Institute of Advanced Study, the Wissenschaftskolleg, the European University Institute, the Bellagio Study and Conference Centre, and other luxurious and desirable facilities between which a global jet-setting élite flits, enjoying academic sabbaticals followed by long summer holidays. One reason is probably that all of this half-intellectual, half-tourist activity takes place overwhelmingly in English, and French academics have switched to English less readily than their colleagues in the north and the south, and even than all their European neighbors. Loyalty to the French language, which has its good side, is also an obstacle to integration into the academic "International." And then – as everyone knows – the great idiosyncrasy of the French university system, which is highly opaque when seen from outside and almost incomprehensible to the uninitiated, discourages partners. Despite recent efforts, such as "Blaise Pascal" chairs financed by the Île-de-France region and the École Normale Supérieure foundation to invite eminent foreign scholars, France is home to few institutions of this kind, which strengthen scholarly networks and communities: it is therefore too far out of the loop. Let us hope that university reform will make it possible for all disciplines to interact, that the creation of foundations will allow universities to raise funds to diversify their activities and open up to the world, that the birth of several Institutes for Advanced Studies, in Paris and Lyon, will make it easier to invite foreign scholars, and that French universities will soon be better incorporated into the global network.[34]

The French will need to change their attitudes – to ensure, for example, that an academic who returns from abroad, or even one who has taken a sabbatical, is not penalized on his return, ragged like some rookie. For this is one of the reasons that, although few sabbaticals are offered, applicants are in no hurry to get them: after one semester of absence, they risk losing all their accrued benefits, their dearly earned privileges – and France is still, in too many ways, a system of privileges, not of rights and duties.

But taking a step back from the marketplace of ideas and talents might not be a bad thing. We are no longer leaders in ideas. We have few global intellectuals, because we negotiated the turning of postcolonialism clumsily. For every Alain Badiou – the last of the *Mao*hicans, the most dogmatic of French philosophers, however urbane – who belatedly broke through onto the big capitalist theater of ideas, how many Slavoj Žižeks, Gayatri Chakravorty Spivaks, and Homi Bhabhas do we find, who have been trained in French thought, who have drawn their earliest intellectual sustenance from Lacan, Foucault, and Derrida, but have long since gone beyond them, sublated them, and surmounted them?

Between the generation of French *maîtres à penser* and that of today's global thinkers, someone like Edward Said has played a defining role. He too was highly susceptible to French culture, but then turned away from it, or was even disgusted by it, once it had disappointed him. Almost every time we had a conversation – for a long time our offices were practically next door at Columbia, and he had played no small part in my invitation to teach there – he returned with increasing bitterness to the poor reception that France had given his work: his *Orientalism* (French translation Seuil, 1978), largely devoted to French erudition in the nineteenth and twentieth centuries, had been coldly received in Paris, and the book that he was later most attached to, *Culture and Imperialism* (French translation Fayard, 2000) was turned down by Le Seuil (the translation appeared only seven years after the American edition, thanks to *Le Monde diploma-tique*, whose advocacy "placed" him). Said was annoyed: why did France remain impervious to his work when it was translated throughout the world? Why was he welcomed with open arms in all capitals, except in Paris? France is provincial, I replied – and I think this is true. But Said still cared about his reception in France, too much so, if you ask me. In the next generation, Paris was written off.

There is a provincialism of Parisian intellectual life, con-fined as it is to the area between the Quartier Latin and Saint-Germain-des-Prés; it always discovers foreign thought belatedly. This delay can sometimes lead to a leap forward, as when we had the revelation of Saussure at least two gen-erations after the linguists had assimilated – and buried – him, whereupon we made him into the prophet of the structuralist turn, thanks to which we turned everything upside down. But more often, such delays merely lead to us reinventing the wheel.

But we need to weigh up the pros and cons. Global intel-lectuals have become stars, "free agents" as they say in Amer-ican professional sport, players whose contracts are no longer bound by exclusivity clauses, and reach astronomical figures. It is a Bourse for ideas and, like the other Bourse, it suffers from the effects of fashion and creates bubbles, which burst like those in the financial world. Each system has its demons, and I have moved around enough not to idealize any of them. The demon of the market affects supposedly noncom-mercial, not-for-profit organizations such as museums, orchestras, and universities in the United States, which some-times resemble, in their marketing methods, the businesses most characterized by the profit motive. But if the demon of American cultural and intellectual life is the market, in France it is the State, with its competitions, its grants, and its privi-leges. The result is a high degree of rigidity in supply and a great difficulty in adapting to demands and needs. Decentral-ization of the cultural State makes matters worse, because it increases the number of intermediaries and fosters the same opaque mechanisms of decision-making. The French system encourages a provincial localism and a Parisian provincialism and, on both sides, clientelism.

We are still, despite Brussels and globalization, in a planned economy of culture, with its "nomenklatura." It is now a question of better placing the cursor between our old Ancien Régime demon and the demon of the market, which also lurks in wait for us in the form of ratings. Nicolas Sarkozy, in his letter on policy (August 1, 2007), requested that the Minister of Culture "ensure that state aid to promote creativity favors a supply that meets public expectations." He asked the Ministry to require that "each subsidized structure account for its actions and the popularity of its operations," that they be obliged to "yield results" and that "automatic renewal of aid and grants" be stopped. He concluded with the recommendation that "every euro spent should be a useful euro." "Popularity," "usefulness": indeed, these references would have worried Malraux, but, ever since Lang, "public expectations" have not been ignored by those who coordinate cultural festivities. We should beware, however, of the perverse effects of "performance indicators," such as when people expect to assess the Minister of Culture on the number of French film entries during the very same season in which the triumph of *Bienvenue chez les Ch'tis* (Welcome to the Sticks), seen by over 20 million viewers by July 2008, was an opportune reminder of the true nature of what people call a good French film.

In a planned economy, moving to the stage of "glasnost" and "perestroika" makes it seem like a good idea to start to evaluate cultural policies on the basis of their democratic outcomes. But there is reason for disquiet when books and reading disappear from the new organizational flow chart of the Ministry of Culture dictated by the RGPP, and when the management responsible for them, distinguished by some great servants of culture such as Jean Gattégno,[ix] is dissolved into a huge General Management for the Development of Media and the Cultural Economy. Books, films, indeed the whole of culture, are immersed in the world of broadcasting, and risk being perceived tomorrow as no more than "cultural industries" and the "art market." Perhaps Donald Morrison was right – just a little premature.

7.

The king is naked and we have been woken with a jolt: so, it seems, we are no longer read, seen, or heard outside the walls of our besieged Gallic village, apart from a Badiou here and there, an old guru taking flight late in the evening, or a Marion Cotillard, imploding after takeoff because of her support for the conspiracy theory. If this picture is exaggerated and therefore unjust, let us still refrain from taking this as an excuse for ignoring the aspects of it that are correct.

As the rules of American journalism always require an emphasis on the bright side – there is nothing like a happy ending, even in a truthful report – Donald Morrison applies balm to our wounded hearts before concluding. French creativity could regenerate, provided that it renounces the universalism that has defined the Republic since 1789, that it recognizes the communities who live in it, that it promotes diversity, equality, and dignity, and resolutely identifies itself as a "black, white, and light-brown" nation.[x]

Having almost put colonialism behind it – despite our nationalist demon, which has recently tempted us to extol its benefits in the law of February 23, 2005,[xi] later repealed – France has become a "multiethnic bazaar of art, music and writing from the banlieues and disparate corners of the non-white world," which would make it a paradise for lovers of foreign cultures. So French culture should stop continually whining about its decline and recharge its batteries in its margins, it should open itself without qualm to globalization: this is the recommendation of Donald Morrison. Adopt the multicultural recipe, "Happy Together," and we shall be saved.

In any case, we did not wait for this prescription to throw ourselves into crossover culture, the only way of existing today. Think of the Palme d'Or at Cannes awarded by an explicitly political jury to *Entre les murs* (The Class) by Laurent Cantet, who, sensing which way the wind is blowing, showed us a multiethnic class and an emancipatory teacher. Or the Nobel Prize-winner, Le Clézio, whose epic novel *Desert* concerns the people of France's North African colonies. But we still need to be careful! As a diasporic, postmodern metropolis, as a world capital for the twenty-first century, Paris will never rival New York, any more than it can rival it in the Stock Exchange or in auctions.

Will we emerge from decline by overhauling schools, reviving reading, introducing arts education at primary level, getting universities to compete, or submitting cultural affairs, internal and external, to economic liberalization? Many critics of the Ministry of Culture – including Marc Fumaroli, Nathalie Heinich, and Antoine de Baecque – are now demanding a return to an active policy of democratization of culture and a strong involvement on the part of schools in achieving that goal. In order to promote art education in schools, the idea of a merger between the Ministries of Culture and Education was floated under the first government of François Fillon, causing concern among cultural intermediaries and all the clients of the Ministry of Culture.

Or should novelists abandon self-referential fiction and minimalism to reconnect with the real world in all its horror and its generosity, in all its complexity and its effervescence? Should French cinema stop constantly telling trivial stories about yuppies in search of love?

A bit of all of this, is surely the answer. Just as we speak of the Kondratieff cycle in economy, there must be cycles of cultural activity: we can bet that we have reached the period of purgation that prepares new growth, and that the great novel of contemporary France is in press, the new *Journey to the End of the Night*.

After all, we still have huge advantages, especially in the United States, and, curiously, Donald Morrison does not have so much as a word to say about them. It is hatred of

France that saves it in America, and from this point of view we can reassure ourselves: we continue to do everything possible to irritate. France is the nation that arouses exasperation, the one that other nations never tire of inveighing against, the one that survives thanks to their aversion to its ignominies. Basically, what is loved about France are all the reasons people have to make this country, always lecturing others, feel ashamed. French culture is the one people love to curse, and we drag so much baggage behind us, we have so many skeletons in the cupboard, that we are not about to be forgotten.

I write this sentence after returning from the exhibition on the collaborationist photographer André Zucca, "The Parisians Under the Occupation" at the Bibliothèque Historique de la Ville de Paris. It was, indeed, a shameful exhibition. As expected, the *International Herald Tribune* devoted a front-page article to it, longer and more complete than all those in the French press.[35] It's easy to summarize one common reaction : "Those French, they don't miss a trick! Still Vichyssois, still Pétainists. In 2008, they exhibit the splendid color photos of the accredited photographer of *Signal,* the Nazi propaganda magazine, as if it were the Belle Époque with all its *douceur de vivre*! One or two yellow stars pass by here and there: it makes a nice touch of color, rhyming with a mug of beer and a bunch of cherries."

What saves us in America, what ensures that we will be talked about for a long time to come, is the Dreyfus affair and long-standing French anti-Semitism, it is Vichy and collaboration, it is colonialism and torture in Algeria, it is, right now, neocolonialism in Africa and racism and Islamophobia in France. Cast your eyes on the program of a conference of American historians or on that of the annual convention of the Modern Language Association. The greater part of the work that still bears on France rummages around among our acts of hypocrisy and intolerance, our infamies and our crimes, from St. Bartholomew's Day and the revocation of the Edict of Nantes to the law on the Islamic scarf or the regular conflagrations in our suburbs.

Trappings of Greatness

Otherwise, we would no longer exist, we would be like the Swiss. Can you imagine any other culture than French culture making the front cover of *Time*, even the European edition? "The death of Belgian culture"? "The death of Serbian culture"? No, France and culture are synonymous, they mean what people love to hate – or indeed what they hate to love, in spite of the Dreyfus Affair, in spite of Vichy, in spite of General Aussaresses, the latest campus celebrity.[xii] This reminds me of my colleague from Geneva who taught in New York for a whole semester. Every day he read the *New York Times* from the first to the last line: there was never a word about Switzerland. Finally, after three or four months, there was an article on the banks of Zurich, which had colluded with the Nazis in laundering the gold stolen from the Jews of Europe. He felt ashamed, but he almost felt relieved.

We have nothing like that to fear. What with the trials of Paul Touvier and Maurice Papon, the friendship of François Mitterrand for René Bousquet, Jean-Marie Le Pen's repeated outbursts on the Holocaust as a "detail," the responsibility of the SNCF, the French national railway company, for the deportations, the reluctance of French museum curators to seek out the rightful owners of works recovered after World War II ... so long as France irritates the world, especially America, we will not be left to ourselves. Of course, this is no reason for us to cultivate our vices and our immorality. But experience seems to prove that people can rest assured that our evil inclinations will continue to express themselves. The real death of French culture on the international scene will be when the world stops loving to hate France; it will be when French culture gives them no more reasons for loving to hate it. So let's not become too virtuous – not that *that's* going to happen in a hurry.

Notes

1 THE DEATH OF FRENCH CULTURE

1 Known for its distinctive red border, *Time* is the world's first and still largest weekly newsmagazine, with a worldwide circulation of nearly 4 million. It was founded in New York in 1923 by Henry Luce and Briton Hadden and is now part of Time Warner Inc., which also owns CNN and the Warner Brothers movie studio. My story appeared in *Time*'s European and Asian editions, which have a combined circulation of 800,000, about 100,000 of that in the U.K. and 60,000 in France.

2 Olivier Poivre d'Arvor, "Lettre à nos amis américains," *Le Monde*, December 20, 2007.

3 Ifop, *Impact du cinéma français a l'étranger*, December 15, 2004.

4 Deborah Solomon, "Continental drift," *New York Times Magazine*, November 20, 2005.

5 Christina Nehring, "Writers in paradise," *New York Times*, December 12, 2004.

6 Elisabeth Vincentelli, "An American novelist scandalizes France," *salon.com*, February 27, 2007.

7 PEN, *To Be Translated or Not to Be*, 2007, p. 17.

8 Esther Allen, ed., *To Be Translated or Not to Be*, PEN, 2007.

9 *The Independent*, December 6, 2007.

10 Nehring, "Writers in paradise."

11   Cited in *Le Figaro Littéraire*, January 19, 2010, p. 8.
12   Quoted in Nehring, "Writers in paradise."
13   Quoted by Charles Bremner, *The Times*, November 18, 2005.
14   *Cahiers du cinéma*, February 2005, p. 14.
15   Alas, it is no longer in France. In a failed attempt to interest Britain's Royal Society in his discovery, Niépce took the photograph to London. There it sat, seemingly lost, until photo-historian Helmut Gernsheim purchased it in 1952 and donated it to the University of Texas, where it remains.
16   "The treacherous medium," *Boston Review*, September–October 2006.
17   "The rise of the 'starchitect,'" *The New Criterion*, December 2007, p. 4.
18   "Vive le rock 'n' roll," *The Independent*, January 14, 2005.
19   Joseph Murrells, *The Book of Golden Disks*, 2nd edition, Barre & Jenkins, 1978.
20   Ibid.
21   Ben Hall, "Sarkozy steals thunder of rivals on left and right," *Financial Times*, January 12, 2008.
22   "Les Misérables on the mend," *Time*, June 15, 1998.
23   PEN, *To Be Translated or Not to Be*.
24   Marie-Estelle Pech, "Darcos appelle les lycéens à s'inscrire en section littéraire," *Le Figaro*, September 7, 2007.
25   John Rockwell, "French culture under socialism," *New York Times*, March 24, 1993.
26   Sébastien Le Fol, "Vers la séparation de la culture et de l'État," *Le Figaro Magazine*, February 10, 2007, pp. 20–21.
27   *Rapport annuel*, Association des critiques et journalists de bande dessinée (ACBD), cited in *Le Figaro*, December 31, 2008, p. 24.
28   *London Review of Books*, September 2, September 23, 2004.
29   Dana Thomas, "Saïd Taghmaoui: from the ghetto to the global screen," *Newsweek*, December 31, 2007, p. 84.
30   Jean-Paul Sartre, "American novelists in French eyes," *The Atlantic Monthly*, August 1946.

2   THE TRAPPINGS OF GREATNESS

1   "Le déclin français vu des États-Unis," *Le Monde*, November 30, 2007.

2   Perry Anderson, "Dégringolade," and "Union sucrée," *London Review of Books*, September 2 and 23, 2004. These were translated into French under the title *La pensée tiède – un regard critique sur la culture française, suivi de "La Pensée réchauffée," réponse de Pierre Nora* (Paris: Seuil, 2005).

3   See Philippe Roger, *The American Enemy: a story of French anti-Americanism*, trans. Sharon Bowman (Chicago, London: University of Chicago Press, 2005).

4   "The Diminishing Canon of French Literature in America," *Stanford French Review* 15(1–2), pp. 103–15, 1991.

5   Jacques de Guillebon, "Richard Millet: 'Le désenchantement ou la grâce'," *La Nef* 187, November 2007.

6   Maryvonne de Saint-Pulgent, "La France, puissance culturelle?," a lecture given to the Société d'études françaises at Basel on September 17, 2007.

7   This idea is far from new: see Olivier Donnat and Denis Cogneau, *Les Pratiques culturelles des Français, 1973–1989* (Paris: La Découverte/La Documentation française, 1990).

8   See Jacques Barrat, *Géopolitique de la francophonie* (Paris: Presses universitaires de France, 1997).

9   See Benoît Duteutre, "Si la France chante en anglais . . .," *Le Figaro*, May 23, 2008.

10 *Rapport d'information [. . .] sur l'accueil des étudiants étrangers – L'Université, un enjeu international pour la France* (Senate, no. 446, June 30, 2005).

11 *Le Monde*, June 8, 2001.

12 Alain Quemin, "Depuis les années 60, ce sont les Américains qui écrivent les pages de l'histoire de l'art," *Télérama*, October 21, 2007.

13 *La Francophonie dans le monde, 2006–2007* (Paris: Nathan, 2007).

14 See Isabelle Vichniac, "Débâcle de la francophonie dans les instances onusiennes," *Le Monde*, December 19, 1998; and the latest *Rapport d'activités, 2004–2006* by the Organisation internationale de la francophonie.

15 Bernard Schlink, *The Reader*, trans. Carol Brown Janeway (London: Phoenix House, 1997). Originally published as *Der Vorleser* (Zurich: Diogenes, 1995). Published in French as *Le Liseur*, trans. Bernard Lortholary (Paris: Gallimard, 1996).

16 W. G. Sebald, *The Emigrants*, trans. Michael Hulse (London: Harvill, 1996). Originally published as *Die Ausgewanderten*

(Frankfurt: Eichborn, 1993). Published in French as *Les Émigrants*, trans. Patrick Charbonneau (Arles: Actes Sud, 1999).

17 W. G. Sebald, *Austerlitz*, trans. Anthea Bell (London: Hamilton, 2001). Originally published as *Austerlitz* (Munich: Hanser, 2001). Published in French as *Austerlitz*, trans. Patrick Charbonneau (Arles: Actes Sud, 2002).

18 *Échanges internationaux d'une selection de biens et services culturels, 1994–2003 – Définir et évaluer le flux du commerce cultural mondial* (Montréal: Institut de statistiques de l'Unesco, 2005).

19 Dominique Schnapper, "De l'État-providence à la démocratie culturelle," *Commentaire* 68, Winter 1994–95.

20 Le Club des 13, *Le Milieu n'est plus un pont mais une faille* (Paris: Stock, 2008).

21 Serge Guilbaut, *Comment New York vola l'idée d'art moderne – Expressionisme abstrait, liberté et guerre froide* (Paris: Jacqueline Chambon, 1988).

22 See Pascale Laborier, "La *Soziokultur* en RFA. D'un enjeu politique à l'institutionnalisation d'une catégorie d'intervention publique," in Vincent Dubois (ed.), *Politiques locales et enjeux culturels – Les Clochers d'une querelle, XIXe-XXe siècles* (Paris: Comité d'histoire du ministère de la Culture/La Documentation française, 1998).

23 Bernard-Henry Lévy, "American talk about the death of French culture says more about them than us," *The Guardian*, December 8, 2007.

24 *Le Figaro*, December 4, 2007.

25 *Le Monde*, December 20, 2007.

26 *Rapport d'information fait [. . .] à la suite d'une mission de contrôle effectué à l'Académie de France à Rome*, Senate, no. 274, April 18, 2001.

27 Adrien Gouteyron, "À quoi sert la villa Médicis?," *Le Monde*, April 4, 2008.

28 Nicole Vulser, "Un rapport critique le choix des films français promus à l'étranger par Unifrance," *Le Monde*, March 16–17, 2008.

29 *Rapport d'information [. . .] fait au nom de la commission des finances*, no. 428, June 30, 2008. See Valérie Sasportas, "Le rayonnement de la France en questions," *Le Figaro*, July 10, 2008.

30 *La Révision générale des politiques publiques*, Conseil de la modernisation des politiques publiques, April 4, 2008.

31 See Patrick Fauconnier, "L'étonnant miracle de l'Alliance française," *Le Nouvel Observateur*, April 3, 2008.

32 According to Senator Gouteyron's July 2008 report, the 375 million euros spent on the French cultural network abroad (144 cultural centres in 2008, as opposed to 173 in 1996, 220 Alliances françaises managed by an expatriate official, 255 other Alliances) need to be compared with the budget of the Cervantes Institute (89 million), the Goethe-Institut (180 million) and the British Council (230 million).

33 The flow chart of the Ministry of Foreign Affairs was revised in March 2009 and the Direction générale de la coopération internationale et du développement (DGCID), which had succeeded, ten years before, the Direction générale des relations culturelles, scientifiques et techniques (DGRCST), was transformed into a new Direction générale de la mondialisation, du développement et des partenariats (DGM). This reorganization coincided with a slump in the financing of French cultural centers and institutes in 2009 (20 percent on average, up to 30 percent in certain posts), and with a reinforcement of the role of Culturesfrance.

34 This was written before the crisis that shook and the strikes that paralyzed a considerable number of French universities in 2008–09 over the reform of the status of academic staff, a crisis that risks reinforcing French isolation on the global academic scene.

35 Meg Bortin, "Photo exhibit shows Paris under Nazi occupation, minus the misery," *International Herald Tribune*, April 25, 2008.

Translator's Notes

i An allusion to the work by the sixteenth-century French poet Joachim Du Bellay, *Deffence et illustration de la langue françoyse*.

ii A government agency whose aim is to promote French culture throughout the world.

iii An army junta seized power in Algiers on the night of May 13, 1958, with the aim of keeping Algeria French; the subsequent politicking ensured the return to power of General De Gaulle and the establishment of the Fifth Republic.

iv   On this day, François Mitterrand beat Valéry Giscard d'Estaing in the race to become President of France.

v   A French magazine, originally devoted mainly to rock music, that now covers all aspects of contemporary culture. Jean-Pierre Raffarin, mentioned in the next lines, was French Prime Minister between 2002 and 2005, under Jacques Chirac.

vi   Henri Massis (d. 1970) was a prolific right-wing Catholic essayist; Charles Maurras (d. 1952) was a Catholic and royalist writer.

vii   '*Touche pas à mon pote!*' was an anti-racist slogan adopted by SOS-Racisme in the 1980s.

viii   These are all research institutes. The Collège de France awards no degrees: its professors present their work in public. The École Pratique de Hautes Études is a higher education institute focused on research. The CNRS (Centre national de la recherche scientifique) is the biggest research centre in France. The IUS (Institut Universitaire de France) fosters academic research, under the aegis of the Ministry for Higher Education. The Pôle de recherche et d'enseignement supérieur (PRES) and the RTRA (Réseaux thématique de recherche avancée) bring together researchers and higher education establishments.

ix   Jean Gattégno (d. 1994) was a leading French intellectual, a specialist in the works of Lewis Carroll and Oscar Wilde, and a significant figure in supporting public libraries and developing the National Book Center.

x   In the original French, a nation that is *black, blanc, beur*: *black* meaning black, and *beur* being the name often used (including by themselves) of children born in France of North African parents.

xi   This law attempted to ensure that French colonialism was depicted in a favorable light.

xii   Paul Aussaresses, who had fought in Algeria, defended the use of torture there in a 2000 interview with *Le Monde*.